The UK
Ninja Double Stack Air Fryer

Cookbook for Beginners

Time-Saving and Delicious Ninja DoubleStack Recipes to Guide You to Cook Efficiently and Make Every Bite Tasty | Full-Colour Edition

Virginia Mares

Fundamentals of the Ninja DoubleStack XL 2-Drawer Air Fryer

The Ninja DoubleStack XL 2-Drawer Air Fryer is designed for maximum versatility and efficiency in the kitchen. Equipped with Ninja's advanced air-frying technology, this air fryer delivers crispy, golden results using little to no oil, making meals healthier without sacrificing flavour. With its large capacity and innovative features, the Ninja DoubleStack XL 2-Drawer Air Fryer simplifies cooking, making it fast, efficient, and delicious.

What is Ninja DoubleStack XL 2-Drawer Air Fryer?

The Ninja DoubleStack XL 2-Drawer Air Fryer is an advanced kitchen appliance designed to bring ease, efficiency, and versatility to home cooking. Unlike traditional air fryers, this innovative model features a dual-drawer system that allows users to cook two separate dishes at the same time. This unique design is ideal for preparing a variety of meals simultaneously, such as roasting vegetables in one drawer while air-frying crispy chicken in the other, making it especially convenient for families or anyone juggling multiple dishes.

What sets the Ninja DoubleStack XL 2-Drawer Air Fryer apart is its vertical, space-saving design. The air fryer's drawers are stacked on top of one another, so it doesn't take up excessive countertop space. This smart layout is perfect for kitchens of any size, making the most of limited counter space without sacrificing capacity. The drawers have a generous combined volume, providing ample room to cook large meals while keeping the footprint compact.

Equipped with a range of cooking functions—Air Fry, Air Broil, Roast, Bake, Reheat, and Dehydrate—the Ninja DoubleStack XL 2-Drawer Air Fryer is capable of more than just air frying. With minimal oil, this air fryer delivers crispy and flavourful results, perfect for healthier meals without sacrificing taste. The two drawers operate independently, allowing users to customise cooking times and temperatures for each drawer, accommodating a variety of recipes and ingredients at once.

The Match Cook function duplicates settings from one drawer to the other, which is ideal for cooking larger quantities of the same dish. For varied recipes, the Smart Finish function synchronises the end time for both drawers, ensuring that different dishes are ready simultaneously. This feature is especially handy for busy cooks who want a smooth, hassle-free mealtime experience. The Smart Finish feature ensures both drawers complete cooking at the same time, making mealtime smoother and more convenient.

With its large capacity, compact upright design, and innovative functions, the Ninja DoubleStack XL 2-Drawer Air Fryer makes it easy to prepare balanced, flavourful meals in half the time. It's a kitchen solution designed for convenience, quality, and variety, ideal for those looking to streamline their cooking routine without compromising on taste or space.

Next, let's learn its control panel, including function buttons and operating buttons.

·Contents·

Introduction

The Colourful Ninja DoubleStack XL 2-Drawer Air Fryer Cookbook is your ultimate companion for unlocking the full potential of your Ninja DoubleStack XL Air Fryer. Designed specifically with UK home cooks in mind, this cookbook brings a vibrant collection of recipes that are as visually appealing as they are delicious. With step-by-step guidance, each recipe has been thoughtfully crafted to make the most of the air fryer's unique dual-drawer design, allowing you to prepare two dishes simultaneously with ease.

Imagine cooking a complete meal—crispy vegetables in one drawer and perfectly seasoned chicken in the other—all while saving precious time in the kitchen. The Ninja DoubleStack XL 2-Drawer Air Fryer's powerful technology and versatile functions open up endless possibilities, from weekday dinners to special family feasts. With recipes ranging from quick, healthy snacks to hearty mains and decadent desserts, there's something for every taste and dietary need.

Each recipe is accompanied by full-colour photographs to inspire and guide you, ensuring that even beginners can achieve mouth-watering results. You'll also find helpful tips and adjustments to suit your family's preferences, including suggestions for alternative ingredients and serving ideas.

Whether you're looking to maintain a healthy lifestyle, satisfy a craving, or impress your loved ones with minimal effort, this cookbook provides the tools and inspiration to create flavour-packed meals in less time. The Colourful Ninja DoubleStack XL 2-Drawer Air Fryer Cookbook is more than a collection of recipes—it's a gateway to enjoyable, efficient cooking that brings vibrant, delicious food to your table.

Function Buttons

♠ **Air Fry:** Achieve perfect crispiness and crunch with minimal to no oil, offering a healthier alternative to traditional frying methods.

♠ **Air Broil:** Add a crispy finish or melt toppings, delivering an irresistible golden-brown exterior.

♠ **Bake:** Effortlessly create baked treats and desserts with precision and consistency using the Bake function.

♠ **Roast:** Transform the air fryer into a roasting oven, ideal for tender meats and flavourful vegetables, perfect for hearty meals.

♠ **Reheat:** Warm up leftovers with a crisp finish, bringing them back to their fresh-out-of-the-oven state for delicious results every time.

♠ **Dehydrate:** Create healthy snacks by drying out meats, fruits, and vegetables with the Dehydrate function.

Operating Buttons

♠ **Zone 1 Control:** Adjust the settings for the top drawer, allowing customisation for perfect results.

♠ **Zone 2 Control:** Manage the output for the bottom drawer to suit your preferred cooking experience.

♠ **TEMP Button:** Adjust the cooking temperature before or during cooking for precision every time.

♠ **TIME Button:** Set or adjust the cooking time, providing full control over the duration of each cooking cycle.

♠ **DOUBLE STACK PRO Button:** Activate DOUBLE STACK PRO to cook up to four foods simultaneously, ideal for diverse meals.

♠ **SMART FINISH Button:** Synchronise the end times for both zones with SMART FINISH, ensuring evenly cooked dishes ready to serve together.

♠ **MATCH COOK Button:** Copy Zone 1 settings to Zone

2 with MATCH COOK, ensuring consistent results across both drawers.

- ♠ **START/PAUSE Button:** Begin or pause cooking with ease by pressing START/PAUSE after selecting your settings.
- ♠ **HOLD Mode:** During SMART FINISH, HOLD mode keeps one Zone on standby while the other continues cooking, synchronising your meal.
- ♠ **STANDBY Mode:** After 10 minutes of inactivity, the unit enters STANDBY mode, conserving energy for peace of mind.

Benefits of Using It

Using he Ninja DoubleStack XL 2-Drawer Air Fryer has many benefits.

1. Efficient Dual-Drawer Cooking

The standout feature of the Ninja DoubleStack XL 2-Drawer Air Fryer is its dual-drawer design, which allows you to cook two different dishes at once. This setup is perfect for preparing meals for the entire family without juggling multiple appliances or waiting for one dish to finish before starting the next. By using each drawer independently, you can cook separate dishes with different cooking times and temperatures simultaneously, saving you time and simplifying meal prep.

2. Space-Saving Vertical Design

Unlike most double-drawer air fryers, the Ninja DoubleStack XL 2-Drawer Air Fryer utilises a clever vertical layout. This upright, compact design takes up less countertop space, making it ideal for smaller kitchens or for those looking to optimise their cooking area. You can enjoy the versatility of a large-capacity air fryer without compromising valuable kitchen space.

3. Multiple Cooking Functions in One Appliance

This air fryer is designed to handle a range of cooking methods beyond simple frying. With functions such as Air Fry, Air Broil, Air Broil, Roast, Bake, Reheat, and Dehydrate, it's a versatile appliance capable of preparing a wide variety of dishes, from crispy chips to tender roasts and even dehydrated fruits. This multifunctional approach not only broadens your culinary options but also reduces the need for multiple gadgets in the kitchen.

4. Healthier Cooking with Minimal Oil

One of the primary benefits of air frying is its ability to create deliciously crispy foods with significantly less oil than traditional frying methods. The Ninja DoubleStack XL 2-Drawer Air Fryer uses powerful, circulating hot air to achieve the same crispy results without excess fat, making it a healthier option for you and your family. It's ideal for those seeking healthier alternatives to deep-fried foods without sacrificing taste and texture.

5. Smart Finish Function for Synchronized Cooking

The Smart Finish feature is a game-changer for those who want perfectly timed meals. When using different cooking functions or settings in each drawer, Smart Finish synchronises the end times, so both drawers complete cooking at the same time. This eliminates the need to monitor or adjust cooking times manually, allowing you to enjoy a seamless, stress-free cooking experience and serve dishes that are ready to eat together.

6. Match Cook for Larger Batches

For instances when you need to prepare larger quantities of the same dish, the Match Cook function is extremely helpful. This feature copies the settings from one drawer to the other, ensuring consistent cooking across both drawers. It's especially useful for large gatherings or meal prepping, where you may want to make a bigger batch of your favourite dish without adjusting settings for each drawer separately.

7. Time-Saving and Convenient

The Ninja DoubleStack XL 2-Drawer Air Fryer dramatically reduces cooking times compared to conventional ovens, thanks to its rapid air circulation technology. This air fryer preheats in seconds and cooks food faster, which means you spend less time waiting for meals to finish. For busy households or those with packed schedules, this quick cooking time makes mealtimes more efficient and convenient.

8. Large Capacity for Family Meals

With a generous total capacity across the two drawers, the Ninja DoubleStack XL 2-Drawer Air Fryer is perfect for family meals or entertaining guests. Whether you're preparing mains and sides simultaneously or cooking for a larger group, the ample space provided by the dual drawers means you can create a variety of dishes with ease. This large capacity ensures you can cook for everyone without needing to run multiple batches.

9. Easy to Use and Clean

The user-friendly control panel and intuitive settings make the Ninja DoubleStack XL 2-Drawer Air Fryer accessible for both beginners and experienced cooks. Each function is clearly labelled, and adjusting settings for temperature, time, and mode is straightforward. Additionally, the non-stick drawers and crisper plates are easy to clean, either by hand or in the dishwasher, saving you time on post-cooking cleanup. The appliance's design also includes a "Cool Down" period after cooking, making it safe to handle once it finishes cooking.

10. Energy-Efficient and Eco-Friendly

Compared to using a conventional oven, the Ninja DoubleStack XL 2-Drawer Air Fryer is more energy-efficient, using less electricity to reach high temperatures and cook food quickly. This not only reduces your energy bills but also minimises the environmental impact of frequent cooking. By using hot air circulation and requiring shorter cooking

times, this air fryer offers an eco-friendly alternative to larger, more energy-intensive kitchen appliances.

In a word, the Ninja DoubleStack XL 2-Drawer Air Fryer combines innovation, efficiency, and convenience, making it a must-have appliance for any kitchen. From its space-saving vertical design to its large capacity and easy cleanup, the Ninja DoubleStack XL 2-Drawer Air Fryer stands out as a versatile, user-friendly, and energy-efficient choice, helping you save time, reduce effort, and enjoy delicious, balanced meals.

Before First Use

1.Remove Packaging: Take off any packaging material, promotional labels, and tape from the unit.

2.Read the Manual: Take out all accessories from the package and read the manual thoroughly. Pay special attention to operating instructions, warnings, and safety measures to avoid any injuries or damage.

3.Wash Components: Clean the drawers, crisper plates, and Stacked Meal Racks in hot, soapy water. Rinse and dry them thoroughly afterward. These parts are dishwasher-safe, but for longevity, hand-washing is recommended.

4.Avoid Dishwasher for Main Unit: NEVER place the main unit in the dishwasher, as it is not dishwasher-safe.

Step-by-Step Use

The Ninja DoubleStack XL 2-Drawer Air Fryer offers a wide range of cooking functions to suit all your culinary needs. Follow this guide for each function, making the most of its dual-drawer capability with Match Cook and Smart Finish features.

Air Fry

♠ **Preparation:** Insert the crisper plate into one of the drawers, place your ingredients in it, and insert the drawer into the air fryer.

♠ **Select Function:** Turn the dial to AIR FRY.

♠ **Adjust Temperature:** Press the TEMP button and use the dial to set the desired temperature.

♠ **Set Cooking Time:** Press the TIME button and adjust the time using the dial.

♠ **Start Cooking:** Press the START/PAUSE button to begin air frying. Shake or turn ingredients halfway through for even crisping if needed.

♠ **Completion:** The unit will beep when cooking is complete. Carefully remove food using silicone-tipped tongs.

Air Broil

♠ **Preparation:** Insert the crisper plate into one of the drawers, place ingredients directly in the drawer, then insert the drawer into the air fryer.

♠ **Select Function:** Turn the dial to AIR BROIL.

♠ **Set Cooking Time:** Press the TIME button and adjust the time. The temperature is preset at 450°F. There is no temperature adjustment available or necessary when using this function.

♠ **Start Cooking:** Press START/PAUSE to begin air broiling. You can watch your food's progress through the cooking time.

♠ **Completion:** The air fryer will beep once finished. Carefully remove food and avoid placing hot drawers on the appliance.

Bake

♠ **Preparation:** Insert the crisper plate into one of the drawers, place your ingredients in it, and insert the drawer into the air fryer.

♠ **Select Function:** Choose BAKE with the dial.

♠ **Adjust Temperature:** Press the TEMP button and adjust as desired. Lower temperature by 25°F when converting from conventional oven recipes.

♠ **Set Cooking Time:** Press the TIME button and set the time as per your recipe.

♠ **Start Cooking:** Press START/PAUSE to begin cooking.

♠ **Completion:** When finished, the air fryer will beep. Carefully remove the food, using mitts if necessary.

Roast

♠ **Preparation:** Insert the crisper plate into one of the drawers, place your ingredients in it, and insert the drawer into the air fryer.

♠ **Select Function:** Use the dial to choose ROAST.

♠ **Adjust Temperature:** Press TEMP and use the dial to set the desired temperature.

♠ **Set Cooking Time:** Press TIME and adjust as necessary for your recipe.

♠ **Start Cooking:** Press START/PAUSE to begin roasting.

♠ **Completion:** The air fryer will signal when roasting is done. Use silicone-tipped utensils to handle food.

Reheat

- ♠ **Preparation:** Insert the crisper plate into one of the drawers, place your ingredients in it, and insert the drawer into the air fryer.
- ♠ **Select Function:** Choose REHEAT using the dial.
- ♠ **Adjust Temperature:** Press TEMP button and set the desired temperature.
- ♠ **Set Time:** Press TIME button and adjust the time as per your recipe.
- ♠ **Start Cooking:** Press START/PAUSE to begin reheating.
- ♠ **Completion:** The air fryer will beep when reheating completes, reviving leftovers to a crispy finish.

Dehydrate

- ♠ **Preparation:** Insert the crisper plate into one of the drawers, place your ingredients in it, and insert the drawer into the air fryer.
- ♠ **Select Function:** Turn the dial to DEHYDRATE.
- ♠ **Adjust Temperature:** Press TEMP button to set the desired dehydration temperature.
- ♠ **Set Time:** Press TIME button and adjust to the recipe's recommended time.
- ♠ **Start Dehydration:** Press START/PAUSE to begin.
- ♠ **Completion:** The unit will beep when dehydration is done. Carefully remove your dried ingredients.

Match Cook

- ♠ **Preparation:** Insert crisper plates in both drawers, place ingredients into both drawers, and insert the drawer in the air fryer.
- ♠ **Set Parameters in Zone 1:** Select your desired function, then set the TEMP and TIME as needed.
- ♠ **Activate Match Cook:** Press the MATCH COOK button to apply the Zone 1 settings to Zone 2, ensuring both drawers have the same settings.
- ♠ **Start Cooking:** Press START/PAUSE to begin cooking in both drawers simultaneously.
- ♠ **Completion:** The air fryer will beep when finished, and both drawers will cool down for 60 seconds. Carefully remove food.

Smart Finish

- ♠ **Preparation:** Insert crisper plates in both drawers, place ingredients into both drawers, and insert the drawer in the air fryer.
- ♠ **Set Zone 1 Parameters:** Select your desired cooking function and adjust the TEMP and TIME settings for Zone 1.
- ♠ **Set Zone 2 Parameters:** Press the Zone 2 button, choose the cooking function, and adjust the TEMP and TIME for Zone 2.

- ♠ **Activate Smart Finish:** Press SMART FINISH to synchronise cooking so both drawers finish simultaneously.
- ♠ **Start Cooking:** Press START/PAUSE to begin.
- ♠ **Completion:** The unit will beep when Smart Finish completes, and the food in both drawers will be ready at the same time.

Here are other tips for using this device.

Using Double Stack Pro

The Double Stack Pro feature lets you cook up to four different foods at once in the two independent drawers. You can choose to cook in both zones or just a single zone, depending on your needs.

Using SMART FINISH or MATCH COOK with Double Stack Pro

Press the DOUBLE STACK PRO button before selecting either SMART FINISH or MATCH COOK functions. If using only one zone, press DOUBLE STACK PRO first, then press START/PAUSE to begin cooking. This ensures efficient air fryer operation.

Pausing Cooking in a Single Zone

To stop cooking in one zone, select the desired zone and press START/PAUSE. To resume, press START/PAUSE again. **(Note on SMART FINISH Mode:** When using SMART FINISH, it's best to pause both zones by pressing START/ PAUSE for synchronised finishing times.)

Ending Cooking Time in One Zone (While Using Both)

Select the zone you want to stop. Press the TIME button and turn the dial to zero. After 3 seconds, "END" will show on the display, and cooking will continue in the other zone.

Tips for Using Accessories

The Ninja DoubleStack XL 2-Drawer Air Fryer is equipped with versatile accessories that can enhance your cooking experience. Here are some tips for maximising their effectiveness and ensuring the best results.

Crisper Plates

- ♠ **Optimal Air Circulation:** Place the crisper plates in each drawer to elevate ingredients, allowing air to circulate evenly around the food for a consistently crispy texture.
- ♠ **Prevent Overcrowding:** Avoid overloading the crisper plates, as it can hinder air circulation and affect cooking performance. Instead, arrange food in a single layer for more uniform results.
- ♠ **Mid-Cooking Shake:** For foods like chips or vegetables, remove the drawer halfway through cooking and shake the contents gently. This helps maintain even crispiness.

Stacked Meal Racks

- ♠ **Multi-Layer Cooking:** When using the Stacked Meal Racks, you can cook different items in each drawer at once, or layer compatible foods within the same drawer, helping you make the most of the dual-zone function.
- ♠ **Ideal Food Types:** The racks are perfect for foods that don't require stirring or turning, such as fish fillets, sliced vegetables, or thin cuts of meat. However, avoid foods that expand significantly during cooking.
- ♠ **Monitor Cooking Times:** Foods placed on the top rack

may cook slightly faster than those on the bottom due to air circulation differences, so monitor them closely to avoid overcooking.

Silicone-Tipped Tongs

♠ **Protect Non-Stick Coating:** Always use silicone-tipped tongs when removing food from the crisper plates or drawers. Metal utensils can scratch or damage the non-stick coating, reducing the lifespan of the accessories.

♠ **Easy Turning:** For foods like chicken wings or breaded items, tongs help you turn pieces halfway through for even cooking without disturbing the food structure.

Using these tips, you can enjoy the versatility and convenience of the Ninja DoubleStack XL 2-Drawer Air Fryer and achieve excellent results with every meal.

Helpful Cooking Tips

1. Arrange Ingredients Evenly: For even browning, place ingredients in a single layer at the bottom of the drawer without overlapping. If they overlap, shake the drawer halfway through the cooking time for best results.

2. Adjust Temperature and Time During Cooking: You can adjust the cooking temperature and time at any stage. Select the Zone you wish to change, then press the TEMP or TIME button and use the dial to modify the settings.

3. Converting Oven Recipes: When converting from conventional oven recipes, lower the temperature by 25°F and monitor food closely to prevent overcooking.

4. Prevent Lightweight Foods from Moving: The air fryer fan may occasionally cause lightweight foods to shift. Secure items (like the top slice of bread on a sandwich) with wooden toothpicks to keep them in place.

5. Start Cooking Immediately: After choosing a cooking function, press START/PAUSE to begin right away. The appliance will operate at the default temperature and time settings.

6. Add Oil for Crispier Vegetables and Potatoes: For optimal results with fresh vegetables and potatoes, add at least 1 tablespoon of oil. Use more if you prefer extra crispiness.

7. Check Cooking Progress: Monitor food during cooking and remove it once it reaches your desired level of brownness. Use an instant-read thermometer to check the internal temperature of meat and fish.

8. Remove Food Promptly: To prevent overcooking, take the food out immediately after the cook time finishes.

Cleaning and Maintenance

Proper cleaning and maintenance of the Ninja DoubleStack XL 2-Drawer Air Fryer will ensure optimal performance and extend its lifespan. Here's a guide to keep your air fryer in excellent condition.

Daily Cleaning Routine

♠ **Allow to Cool:** Always let the air fryer cool completely before beginning any cleaning routine. This ensures safety and prevents damage to components.

♠ **Remove Accessories:** Take out both crisper plates, drawers, and any other accessories from the unit.

♠ **Wash Accessories:** The crisper plates, drawers, and meal

racks are dishwasher-safe, but for a longer lifespan, hand-wash them in warm, soapy water. Use a soft sponge or cloth to avoid scratching the non-stick surface, then rinse and dry thoroughly.

♠ **Cleaning the Drawer Compartments:** If any food spills inside the drawer compartments, wipe them with a damp cloth to remove residue. Avoid soaking any parts of the main unit in water.

Cleaning the Main Unit

♠ **Wipe Exterior:** Use a soft, damp cloth to clean the exterior of the air fryer. Avoid using abrasive sponges, as these can damage the finish.

♠ **Control Panel Care:** Gently wipe the control panel with a damp, lint-free cloth. Avoid spraying water or cleaner directly onto the panel, as excess moisture can seep inside and cause malfunctions.

♠ **Cleaning the Interior:** Occasionally, food particles may collect in the main cavity. Wipe the inside with a soft, damp cloth to keep it clear of residue.

Dealing with Grease and Stubborn Residue

♠ **Soak Accessories:** For stuck-on grease, soak the crisper plates and drawers in warm, soapy water for 10–15 minutes. This will loosen any residue, making it easier to clean.

♠ **Non-Abrasive Cleaner:** If necessary, use a non-abrasive cleaner and a soft brush to scrub away any remaining residue on the accessories. Avoid harsh chemicals, as these can damage the non-stick coating.

Regular Maintenance Tips

♠ **Check for Build-up:** Periodically check the fan and heating element for build-up of grease or food particles. A damp cloth can usually clear these areas, but avoid water dripping directly onto the heating element.

♠ **Inspect the Power Cord:** Regularly examine the power cord for any signs of wear or damage. If the cord shows any issues, discontinue use until it's been inspected by a qualified technician.

Storage Advice

♠ **Keep Dry and Upright:** Store your air fryer in a dry place, keeping it upright to prevent any internal damage.

♠ **Avoid Excessive Dust Exposure:** If storing for an extended period, cover the air fryer to keep dust away from the control panel and heating elements.

Following these cleaning and maintenance steps will ensure your Ninja DoubleStack XL 2-Drawer Air Fryer remains in peak condition, delivering consistent, delicious results for years to come.

Frequently Asked Questions

1. Can I cook different foods in each drawer simultaneously?
Yes, the Ninja DoubleStack XL 2-Drawer Air Fryer allows you to cook two different foods at once, each with separate temperature and time settings. Use the SMART FINISH function to ensure both drawers finish cooking simultaneously, even if they have different cooking times.

2. How do I clean the drawers and accessories?
The crisper plates, drawers, and other accessories are dishwasher-safe. However, for longer-lasting results, it's recommended to hand-wash them in warm, soapy water with a soft cloth. Ensure they are fully dried before reinserting into the air fryer.

3. What is the MATCH COOK function, and how does it work?
The MATCH COOK function allows you to set identical temperature and time for both drawers, making it ideal for cooking larger portions of the same food. Simply select MATCH COOK after setting the temperature and time in one zone, and the settings will automatically apply to the second drawer.

4. Do I need to preheat the air fryer before cooking?
Preheating is generally not necessary with the Ninja DoubleStack XL 2-Drawer Air Fryer. However, if your recipe specifies preheating, you can run the unit on a quick cycle before adding ingredients to bring it up to temperature.

5. What should I do if lightweight foods blow around in the air fryer?
Lightweight items, like thin slices of bread or herbs, can sometimes move due to the air circulation. To prevent this, secure foods with wooden toothpicks or lightly press them into the crisper plate. This will help keep them in place during cooking.

6. What's the best way to prevent food from sticking?
Lightly coat the crisper plates or drawers with oil before cooking, especially for foods prone to sticking, such as marinated items or breaded vegetables. Avoid using aerosol sprays, as they may damage the non-stick surface.

7. Can I use both drawers without activating Double Stack Pro?
Yes, you can operate each drawer independently without Double Stack Pro. Double Stack Pro is helpful when you need to synchronise cooking in both zones or maximise space for larger meal portions.

8. How do I stop the cooking cycle early?
To stop cooking, press START/PAUSE and then the POWER button to turn off the unit. Opening the drawer will also pause the cooking, allowing you to check food without resetting the timer.

9. Is it safe to leave the air fryer plugged in when not in use?
While the Ninja DoubleStack XL 2-Drawer Air Fryer enters Standby Mode after 10 minutes of inactivity, it's always a good practice to unplug the unit for safety and energy conservation when not in use.

10. Can I use aluminium foil or parchment paper in the air fryer?
Yes, you can use aluminium foil or parchment paper, but make sure it doesn't block airflow within the drawer. Place it beneath the food to prevent sticking or make clean-up easier. Avoid covering the entire crisper plate or drawer, as this may affect cooking performance.

4-Week Meal Plan

Week 1

Day 1:
Breakfast: Classic Denver Omelet
Lunch: Crispy Brussels Sprouts
Snack: Crispy Kale Chips
Dinner: Jalapeño Popper Hasselback Chicken
Dessert: Keto Pecan Snowball Cookies

Day 2:
Breakfast: Low-Carb Chocolate Chip Muffins
Lunch: Burrata Stuffed Tomatoes
Snack: Savoury Ranch Chicken Bites
Dinner: Healthy Carne Asada
Dessert: Halle Berries and Cream Cobbler

Day 3:
Breakfast: Mini Cinnamon Biscuits
Lunch: Garlic Parmesan Roasted Cauliflower
Snack: Reuben Egg Rolls
Dinner: Healthy Shrimp Scampi
Dessert: Mixed Berry Hand Pies

Day 4:
Breakfast: Tasty Meritage Eggs
Lunch: Bacon Wrapped Asparagus
Snack: Simple Cauliflower Tots
Dinner: Classic Chicken Kiev
Dessert: Low-Carb Chocolate Doughnut Holes

Day 5:
Breakfast: Gyro Breakfast Patties with Tzatziki Sauce
Lunch: Mac and Cheese
Snack: Savoury Tomatoes Provençal
Dinner: Cheeseburger Meatballs
Dessert: Tasty Olive Oil Cake

Day 6:
Breakfast: Keto Breakfast Quiche
Lunch: Easy Fluffy Pancake
Snack: Two-Ingredient Cheese Crisps
Dinner: Simple Sesame-Crusted Tuna Steak
Dessert: Decadent Chocolate Soufflés

Day 7:
Breakfast: Simple Mexican Shakshuka
Lunch: Spinach and Cheese Frittata
Snack: Crispy Onion Rings
Dinner: Herbed Lamb Chops
Dessert: Sweet Cream Cheese Shortbread Cookies

Week 2

Day 1:
Breakfast: Banana Walnut Cake
Lunch: Courgette & Cauliflower Fritters
Snack: Bacon-Wrapped Jalapeño Poppers
Dinner: Chicken Cordon Bleu Meatballs
Dessert: Air-Fried Cinnamon Doughnut Bites

Day 2:
Breakfast: Spinach and Feta Egg Bake
Lunch: Buttery Green Beans
Snack: Homemade French Fries
Dinner: Salisbury Steak with Mushroom Onion Gravy
Dessert: Chocolate Mayo Cake

Day 3:
Breakfast: Crunchy Keto Granola
Lunch: Classic Aubergine Lasagna
Snack: Parmesan-Rosemary Roasted Radishes
Dinner: Crispy Crab Rangoon Patties with Sweet and Sour Sauce
Dessert: Mouthwatring S'mores Pockets

Day 4:
Breakfast: Roasted Vegetable Frittata
Lunch: Crispy Fried Green Tomato Salad with Buttermilk Dressing
Snack: Spinach and Artichoke Stuffed Mushrooms
Dinner: Thanksgiving Turkey Breast
Dessert: Glazed Cherry Turnovers with Almonds

Day 5:
Breakfast: Bacon Puff Pastry Pinwheels
Lunch: Roasted Broccoli with Balsamic Sesame Dressing
Snack: Crispy Spicy Tofu
Dinner: Zesty Black and Blue Burgers
Dessert: Keto Pecan Snowball Cookies

Day 6:
Breakfast: Classic Denver Omelet
Lunch: Crispy Brussels Sprouts
Snack: Savoury Ranch Chicken Bites
Dinner: Easy Pecan-Crusted Catfish
Dessert: Molten Chocolate Almond Cakes

Day 7:
Breakfast: Low-Carb Chocolate Chip Muffins
Lunch: Burrata Stuffed Tomatoes
Snack: Crispy Kale Chips
Dinner: Chinese Five-Spice Pork Belly
Dessert: Halle Berries and Cream Cobbler

Week 3	Week 4

Week 3

Day 1:
Breakfast: Mini Cinnamon Biscuits
Lunch: Garlic Parmesan Roasted Cauliflower
Snack: Reuben Egg Rolls
Dinner: The Best Popcorn Chicken
Dessert: Low-Carb Chocolate Doughnut Holes

Day 2:
Breakfast: Tasty Meritage Eggs
Lunch: Bacon Wrapped Asparagus
Snack: Simple Cauliflower Tots
Dinner: Ground Beef Taco Rolls
Dessert: Decadent Chocolate Soufflés

Day 3:
Breakfast: Keto Breakfast Quiche
Lunch: Mac and Cheese
Snack: Savoury Tomatoes Provençal
Dinner: Nutritious Fish Taco Bowl
Dessert: Sweet Cream Cheese Shortbread Cookies

Day 4:
Breakfast: Gyro Breakfast Patties with Tzatziki Sauce
Lunch: Spinach and Cheese Frittata
Snack: Two-Ingredient Cheese Crisps
Dinner: Garlic Parmesan Turkey Meatballs
Dessert: Tasty Olive Oil Cake

Day 5:
Breakfast: Banana Walnut Cake
Lunch: Easy Fluffy Pancake
Snack: Crispy Onion Rings
Dinner: Parmesan-Crusted Steak
Dessert: Mouthwatring S'mores Pockets

Day 6:
Breakfast: Simple Mexican Shakshuka
Lunch: Courgette & Cauliflower Fritters
Snack: Bacon-Wrapped Jalapeño Poppers
Dinner: Tender Scallops with Lemon-Butter Sauce
Dessert: Air-Fried Cinnamon Doughnut Bites

Day 7:
Breakfast: Spinach and Feta Egg Bake
Lunch: Buttery Green Beans
Snack: Homemade French Fries
Dinner: Pork Kebabs with Bell Peppers and Onions
Dessert: Mixed Berry Hand Pies

Week 4

Day 1:
Breakfast: Crunchy Keto Granola
Lunch: Classic Aubergine Lasagna
Snack: Parmesan-Rosemary Roasted Radishes
Dinner: Chicken Strips with Satay Sauce
Dessert: Glazed Cherry Turnovers with Almonds

Day 2:
Breakfast: Roasted Vegetable Frittata
Lunch: Crispy Fried Green Tomato Salad with Buttermilk Dressing
Snack: Spinach and Artichoke Stuffed Mushrooms
Dinner: Delicious Bacon Cheeseburger Meatloaf
Dessert: Chocolate Mayo Cake

Day 3:
Breakfast: Bacon Puff Pastry Pinwheels
Lunch: Roasted Broccoli with Balsamic Sesame Dressing
Snack: Crispy Spicy Tofu
Dinner: Cajun Salmon Burgers
Dessert: Keto Pecan Snowball Cookies

Day 4:
Breakfast: Classic Denver Omelet
Lunch: Crispy Brussels Sprouts
Snack: Crispy Kale Chips
Dinner: Air-Fried Chicken Paillard
Dessert: Halle Berries and Cream Cobbler

Day 5:
Breakfast: Low-Carb Chocolate Chip Muffins
Lunch: Burrata Stuffed Tomatoes
Snack: Two-Ingredient Cheese Crisps
Dinner: Steak Fajitas with Vegetables
Dessert: Molten Chocolate Almond Cakes

Day 6:
Breakfast: Mini Cinnamon Biscuits
Lunch: Garlic Parmesan Roasted Cauliflower
Snack: Savoury Ranch Chicken Bites
Dinner: Lemon-Garlic Tilapia Fillets
Dessert: Low-Carb Chocolate Doughnut Holes

Day 7:
Breakfast: Tasty Meritage Eggs
Lunch: Bacon Wrapped Asparagus
Snack: Homemade French Fries
Dinner: Crispy Pork Chops
Dessert: Decadent Chocolate Soufflés

Chapter 1 Breakfast

Classic Denver Omelet

⏰ **Prep Time:** 5 minutes 🍳 **Cook:** 8 minutes 🍽 **Serves:** 1

2 large eggs
60ml unsweetened, unflavoured almond milk
¼ teaspoon fine sea salt
⅛ teaspoon ground black pepper
30g diced ham (omit for vegetarian)
30g diced green and red bell peppers
2 tablespoons diced green onions, plus more for garnish
30g shredded cheddar cheese (omit for dairy-free)
Quartered cherry tomatoes, for serving (optional)

1. Grease a cake pan that fits your air fryer and set aside. 2. In a small bowl, use a fork to whisk together the eggs, almond milk, salt, and pepper. Add the ham, bell peppers, and green onions. Pour the mixture into the greased pan. Add the cheese on top (if using). 3. Insert a crisper plate in a drawer, place the pan in the drawer, and insert the drawer in the unit. 4. Select Zone 1 and turn the dial to select AIR FRY. Set the cooking temperature to 175°C and cook time to 8 minutes. Press the START/PAUSE button to begin cooking. Cook until the eggs are cooked to your liking. 5. Loosen the omelet from the sides of the pan with a spatula and place it on a serving plate. Garnish with the green onions and serve with the cherry tomatoes, if desired. Best served fresh.

Gyro Breakfast Patties with Tzatziki Sauce

⏰ **Prep Time:** 10 minutes 🍳 **Cook:** 20 minutes 🍽 **Serves:** 4

Patties:
910g ground lamb or beef
55g diced red onions
30g sliced black olives
2 tablespoons tomato sauce
1 teaspoon dried oregano leaves
1 teaspoon Greek seasoning
2 cloves garlic, minced
1 teaspoon fine sea salt
Tzatziki Sauce:
230g full-fat sour cream
1 small cucumber, chopped
½ teaspoon fine sea salt
½ teaspoon garlic powder, or 1 clove garlic, minced
¼ teaspoon dried dill weed, or 1 teaspoon finely chopped fresh dill
For Garnish/Serving:
55g crumbled feta cheese
Diced red onions
Sliced black olives
Sliced cucumbers

1. Place the ground lamb, onions, olives, oregano, Greek seasoning, garlic, tomato sauce, and salt in a large bowl. Mix well to combine the ingredients. 3. Using your hands, form the mixture into sixteen 3-inch patties. 4. Insert a crisper plate in the bottom of drawer. Add the patties in each drawer. Place a Stacked Meal Rack in each drawer over the patties. 5. Place the patties on one rack and insert the drawer in Zone 1. Place the patties on the other rack and insert the drawer in Zone 2. Insert the drawers in the unit. 6. Select DOUBLE STACK PRO. Select Zone 1, select AIR FRY, and set temperature to 175°C and time to 20 minutes. Select MATCH COOK, and then press START/PAUSE to begin cooking. Cook, flipping halfway through the cooking time. 7. Remove the patties and place them on a serving platter. 8. While the patties cook, make the tzatziki by placing all the ingredients in a small bowl and stirring well. Cover and store in the fridge until ready to serve. Garnish with the ground black pepper before serving. 9. Serve the patties with a dollop of tzatziki, a sprinkle of crumbled feta cheese, diced red onions, sliced black olives, and sliced cucumbers. 10. Store leftovers in an airtight container in the refrigerator for up to 5 days or in the freezer for up to a month. Reheat the patties in a preheated 200°C air fryer for a few minutes, until warmed through.

Mini Cinnamon Biscuits

⏰ **Prep Time: 15 minutes**   🍲 **Cook: 13 minutes**   🍲 **Serves: 4**

220g blanched almond flour
55g Swerve confectioners'-style sweetener or equivalent amount of liquid or powdered sweetener
1 teaspoon baking powder
½ teaspoon fine sea salt
55g plus 2 tablespoons (¾ stick) very cold unsalted butter
60ml unsweetened, unflavoured almond milk
1 large egg
1 teaspoon vanilla extract
3 teaspoons ground cinnamon

Glaze:
55g Swerve confectioners'-style sweetener or equivalent amount of powdered sweetener
60g heavy cream or unsweetened, unflavoured almond milk

1. Insert the crisper plates in each drawer and line the drawers with parchment paper. 2. In a medium-sized bowl, mix together the almond flour, baking powder, sweetener (if powdered; do not add liquid sweetener), and salt. Cut the butter into ½-inch squares, then use a hand mixer to work the butter into the dry ingredients. When you are done, the mixture should still have chunks of butter. 3. In a small bowl, whisk together the almond milk, egg, and vanilla extract (if using liquid sweetener, add it as well) until blended. Using a fork, stir the wet ingredients into the dry ingredients until large clumps form. Add the cinnamon and use your hands to swirl it into the dough. 4. Form the dough into sixteen 1-inch balls and place them on the prepared drawers, spacing them about ½ inch apart. Insert the drawers in the unit. 5. Select Zone 1 and turn the dial to select BAKE. Set the cooking temperature to 175°C and cook time to 10 minutes. Press the MATCH COOK button to copy Zone 1's settings to Zone 2. Press START/PAUSE to begin cooking in both zones. Bake until golden, 10 to 13 minutes. 6. Remove the biscuits from the drawers and let cool on a pan for at least 5 minutes. 7. While the biscuits bake, make the glaze by placing the powdered sweetener in a small bowl and slowly stirring in the heavy cream with a fork. 8. When the biscuits have cooled somewhat, dip the tops into the glaze, allow it to dry a bit, and then dip again for a thick glaze. 9. Serve warm or at room temperature. 10 Store the unglazed biscuits in an airtight container in the refrigerator for up to 3 days or in the freezer for up to a month. Reheat in a preheated 175°C air fryer for 5 minutes, or until warmed through, and dip in the glaze as instructed above.

Tasty Meritage Eggs

⏰ **Prep Time: 5 minutes**   🍲 **Cook: 8 minutes**   🍲 **Serves: 2**

2 teaspoons unsalted butter (or coconut oil for dairy-free), for greasing the ramekins
4 large eggs
2 teaspoons chopped fresh thyme
½ teaspoon fine sea salt
¼ teaspoon ground black pepper
2 tablespoons heavy cream (or unsweetened, unflavoured almond milk for dairy-free)
3 tablespoons finely grated Parmesan cheese (or Kite Hill brand chive cream cheese style spread, softened, for dairy-free)
Fresh thyme leaves, for garnish (optional)

1. Grease two 115g ramekins with the butter. 2. Crack 2 eggs into each ramekin and divide the thyme, salt, and pepper between the ramekins. Pour 1 tablespoon of the heavy cream into each ramekin. Sprinkle each ramekin with 1½ tablespoons of the Parmesan cheese. 3. Insert a crisper plate in a drawer, place the ramekins in the drawer, and insert the drawer in the unit. 4. Select Zone 1 and turn the dial to select AIR FRY. Set the cooking temperature to 200°C and cook time to 8 minutes. Press the START/PAUSE button to begin cooking. Cook for soft-cooked yolks (longer if you desire a harder yolk). 5. Garnish with a sprinkle of ground black pepper and thyme leaves, if desired. Best served fresh.

Simple Mexican Shakshuka

Time: 5 minutes   Cook: 6 minutes   Serves: 1

, room temperature
fine sea salt
smoked paprika
ground cumin
h:
ns cilantro leaves

salsa in a pie pan or a casserole dish that will fit into
er. Crack the eggs into the salsa and sprinkle them with
aprika, and cumin. 2. Insert a crisper plate in a drawer,
e pan in the drawer, and insert the drawer in the unit. 3.
e 1 and turn the dial to select AIR FRY. Set the cooking
e to 200°C and cook time to 6 minutes. Press the START/
utton to begin cooking. Cook until the egg whites are set
lks are cooked to your liking. 4. Remove from the drawer
h with the cilantro before serving. Best served fresh.

Banana Walnut Cake

⏱ Prep Time: 15 minutes   🍞 Cook: 25 minutes   ❧ Serves: 6

110g blanched finely ground almond flour
95g powdered erythritol
2 tablespoons ground golden flaxseed
2 teaspoons baking powder
½ teaspoon ground cinnamon
55g unsalted butter, melted
2½ teaspoons banana extract
1 teaspoon vanilla extract
55g full-fat sour cream
2 large eggs
30g chopped walnuts

1. In a large bowl, mix almond flour, flaxseed, baking powder,
erythritol, and cinnamon. 2. Stir in butter, vanilla extract, banana
extract, and sour cream. 3. Add eggs to the mixture and gently stir
until fully combined. Stir in the walnuts. 4. Pour the mixture into
a nonstick cake pan that fits your air fryer. 5. Insert a crisper plate
in a drawer, place the cake pan in the drawer, and insert the drawer
in the unit. Select Zone 1 and turn the dial to select BAKE. Set the
cooking temperature to 150°C and cook time to 25 minutes. Press
the START/PAUSE button to begin cooking. 6. Cake will be golden
and a toothpick inserted in centre will come out clean when fully
cooked. Allow to fully cool to avoid crumbling. Serve and enjoy.

Low-Carb Chocolate Chip Mu

⏰ **Prep Time:** 5 minutes 🍲 **Cook:** 15 minutes 🍽 **Serves:** 3

165g blanched finely ground almond flour
65g granular brown erythritol
4 tablespoons salted butter, melted
2 large eggs, whisked
1 tablespoon baking powder
80g low-carb chocolate chips

1. In a large bowl, combine all ingredients. Evenly pour the batter into six silicone muffin cups greased with cooking spray. 2. Place bottom layer of muffin cups in the drawer. Insert the Stacked Meal Rack and place the top layer of muffin cups on top. Insert the drawer in the unit. 3. Select DOUBLE STACK PRO. Select Zone 1, select AIR FRY, and set temperature to 160°C and time to 15 minutes. Press the START/PAUSE button to begin cooking. Muffins will be golden brown when done. 4. Let the muffins cool in the cups for 15 minutes to avoid crumbling. Serve warm.

⏰ **Prep T**

130g salsa
2 large eggs
½ teaspoon
¼ teaspoon
⅛ teaspoon
For Garni
2 tablespoo

1. Place th
your air fr
the salt, p
place the
Select Zo
temperatu
PAUSE b
and the y
and garni

Keto Breakfast Quiche

⏰ **Prep Time:** 10 minutes 🍲 **Cook**

Crust:
140g blanched almond flour
110g grated Parmesan or Gouda cheese
¼ teaspoon fine sea salt
1 large egg, beaten
Filling:
120ml chicken or beef broth (or vegetabl
115g shredded Swiss cheese
115g cream cheese
1 tablespoon unsalted butter, melted
4 large eggs, beaten
65g minced leeks or sliced green onions
¾ teaspoon fine sea salt
⅛ teaspoon cayenne pepper
Chopped green onions, for garnish

1. Grease a pie pan that fits your air fryer
of parchment paper with the avocado o
countertop. 2. Make the crust. In a medium-
cheese, flour, and salt and mix well. Add th
dough is well combined and stiff. 3. Place th
one of the greased pieces of parchment. Top
parchment. Using a rolling pin, roll out the d
half of ⅛ inch thick. 4. Press the pie crust int
Insert a crisper plate in a drawer, place the

and insert the drawer in the unit. 5. Select Zone 1 and turn the dial to select BAKE. Set the cooking temperature to 160°
minutes. Press the START/PAUSE button to begin cooking. Bake until it starts to lightly brown. 6. While the crust bakes,
large bowl, combine the broth, cream cheese, Swiss cheese, and butter. Stir in the eggs, salt, leeks, and cayenne pepper. W
pour the mixture into the crust. 7. Place the quiche in the drawer and bake for 15 minutes. Turn the heat down to 150°C an
minutes, or until a knife inserted 1 inch from the edge comes out clean. You may have to cover the edges of the crust with foil
Let the quiche cool for 10 minutes before garnishing it with the chopped green onions and cutting it into wedges. 9. Store l
container in the refrigerator for up to 4 days or in the freezer for up to a month. Reheat in a preheated 175°C air fryer for
warmed through.

Spinach and Feta Egg Bake

⏰ **Prep Time:** 7 minutes   🍲 **Cook:** 23-25 minutes   🗂 **Serves:** 2

Avocado oil spray
40g diced red onion
190g frozen chopped spinach, thawed and drained
4 large eggs
60g heavy (whipping) cream
Sea salt
Freshly ground black pepper
¼ teaspoon cayenne pepper
60g crumbled feta cheese
25g shredded Parmesan cheese

1. Spray a deep air fryer–safe pan that fits your air fryer with oil and put the onion in the pan. 2. Insert a crisper plate in a drawer, place the pan in the drawer, and insert the drawer in the unit. 3. Select Zone 1 and turn the dial to select BAKE. Set the cooking temperature to 175°C and cook time to 7 minutes. Press the START/ PAUSE button to begin cooking. 4. In a medium bowl, beat the eggs, salt, black pepper, heavy cream, and cayenne. 5. Sprinkle the spinach over the onion and pour the egg mixture over the vegetables. 6. Top with the feta and Parmesan cheese. Cook for 16 to 18 minutes, until the eggs are set and lightly brown. 7. Serve and enjoy.

Crunchy Keto Granola

⏰ **Prep Time:** 15 minutes   🍲 **Cook:** 60 minutes   🗂 **Serves:** 4

60g pecans, coarsely chopped
60g walnuts or almonds, coarsely chopped
15g unsweetened flaked coconut
30g almond flour
35g ground flaxseed or chia seeds
2 tablespoons sunflower seeds
2 tablespoons melted butter
30g Swerve sugar replacement
½ teaspoon ground cinnamon
½ teaspoon vanilla extract
¼ teaspoon ground nutmeg
¼ teaspoon salt
2 tablespoons water

1. Cut a piece of parchment paper to fit inside the air fryer drawer. 2. In a large bowl, toss the nuts, coconut, ground flaxseed or chia seeds, sunflower seeds, almond flour, butter, Swerve, cinnamon, nutmeg, salt, vanilla, and water until thoroughly combined. 3. Spread the granola on the parchment paper and flatten to an even thickness. 4. Insert a crisper plate in a drawer, place the parchment paper in the drawer, and insert the drawer in the unit. 5. Select Zone 1 and turn the dial to select AIR FRY. Set the cooking temperature to 120°C and cook time to 60 minutes. Press the START/PAUSE button to begin cooking. Air fry for about an hour, or until golden throughout. 6. Remove the granola from the drawer and allow to fully cool. Break the granola into bite-size pieces and store in a covered container for up to a week.

Roasted Vegetable Frittata

🕐 **Prep Time: 6 minutes** 🍲 **Cook: 13 minutes** 🍂 **Serves: 1-2**

½ red or green bell pepper, cut into ½-inch chunks
4 button mushrooms, sliced
60g diced courgette
½ teaspoon chopped fresh oregano or thyme
1 teaspoon olive oil
3 eggs, beaten
55g grated Cheddar cheese
Salt and freshly ground black pepper, to taste
1 teaspoon butter
1 teaspoon chopped fresh parsley

1. Toss the peppers, mushrooms, courgette, and oregano with the olive oil. 2. Insert a crisper plate in a drawer, place the vegetables in the drawer, and insert the drawer in the unit. 3. Select Zone 1 and turn the dial to select AIR FRY. Set the cooking temperature to 200°C and cook time to 6 minutes. Press the START/PAUSE button to begin cooking. Shake the drawer once or twice during the cooking process to redistribute the ingredients. 4. While the vegetables are cooking, beat the eggs well in a bowl, stir in the Cheddar cheese and season with the salt and freshly ground black pepper. Add the air-fried vegetables to this bowl when they have finished cooking. 5. Place a non-stick metal cake pan that fits your air fryer into the drawer with the butter. Air-fry for 1 minute at 195°C to melt the butter. Remove the cake pan and rotate the pan to distribute the butter and grease the pan. Pour the egg mixture into the cake pan and return the pan to the drawer. 6. Air-fry at 195°C for 12 minutes, or until the frittata has puffed up and is lightly browned. 7. Let the frittata sit in the air fryer for 5 minutes to cool to an edible temperature and set up. Remove the cake pan from the air fryer, sprinkle with the parsley, and serve immediately.

Bacon Puff Pastry Pinwheels

🕐 **Prep Time: 10 minutes** 🍲 **Cook: 10 minutes** 🍂 **Serves: 4**

1 sheet of puff pastry
2 tablespoons maple syrup
45g brown sugar
8 slices bacon (not thick cut)
Coarsely cracked black pepper
Vegetable oil

1. On a lightly floured surface, roll the puff pastry out into a square that measures roughly 10 inches wide by however long your bacon strips are (usually about 11 inches). Cut the pastry into eight even strips. 2. Brush the strips of pastry with the maple syrup and sprinkle the brown sugar on top, leaving 1 inch of dough exposed at the far end of each strip. Place a slice of bacon on each strip of puff pastry, letting ⅛-inch of the length of bacon hang over the edge of the pastry. Season generously with coarsely ground black pepper. 3. With the exposed end of the pastry strips away from you, roll the bacon and pastry strips up into pinwheels. Dab a little water on the exposed end of the pastry and pinch it to the pinwheel to seal the pastry shut. 4. Insert a crisper plate in a drawer and brush or spray the drawer with a little vegetable oil. Place the pinwheels in the drawer and insert the drawer in the unit. 5. Select Zone 1 and turn the dial to select AIR FRY. Set the cooking temperature to 180°C and cook time to 8 minutes. Press the START/PAUSE button to begin cooking. 6. Turn the pinwheels over and air-fry for another 2 minutes to brown the bottom. 7. Serve warm.

Chapter 2 Vegetables and Sides

Crispy Brussels Sprouts

⏰ Prep Time: 5 minutes 🍲 Cook: 8 minutes 🥬 Serves: 4

170g Brussels sprouts, trimmed and halved
3 tablespoons ghee or coconut oil, melted
1 teaspoon fine sea salt or smoked salt
Dash of lime or lemon juice
Thinly sliced Parmesan cheese, for serving (optional; omit for dairy-free)
Lemon slices, for serving (optional)

1. Insert a crisper plate in a drawer and spray the drawer with the avocado oil. 2. In a large bowl, mix together the Brussels sprouts, ghee, and salt. Add the lime or lemon juice. 3. Place the Brussels sprouts in the drawer and insert the drawer in the unit. 4. Select Zone 1 and turn the dial to select AIR FRY. Set the cooking temperature to 200°C and cook time to 8 minutes. Press the START/PAUSE button to begin cooking. Cook until crispy, shaking the drawer after 5 minutes. Serve with the thinly sliced Parmesan and lemon slices, if desired. 5. Best served fresh. Store leftovers in an airtight container in the fridge for up to 5 days. Reheat in a preheated 200°C air fryer for 3 minutes, or until heated through.

Burrata Stuffed Tomatoes

⏰ Prep Time: 5 minutes 🍲 Cook: 5 minutes 🥬 Serves: 4

4 medium tomatoes
½ teaspoon fine sea salt
4 (55g) Burrata balls
Fresh basil leaves, for garnish
Extra-virgin olive oil, for drizzling

1. Core the tomatoes and scoop out the seeds and membranes using a melon baller or spoon. Sprinkle the insides of the tomatoes with the salt. 2. Stuff each tomato with a ball of Burrata. 3. Insert a crisper plate in a drawer, place the tomatoes in the drawer, and insert the drawer in the unit. 4. Select Zone 1 and turn the dial to select ROAST. Set the cooking temperature to 150°C and cook time to 5 minutes. Press the START/PAUSE button to begin cooking. Cook until the cheese has softened. 5. Garnish with the basil leaves and drizzle with the olive oil. Serve warm. 6. Best served fresh. Store leftovers in an airtight container in the refrigerator for up to 4 days. Reheat in a preheated 150°C air fryer for about 3 minutes, until heated through.

Garlic Parmesan Roasted Cauliflower

⏱ **Prep Time:** 5 minutes   🍴 **Cook:** 15 minutes   🍂 **Serves:** 6

1 medium head cauliflower, leaves and core removed, cut into florets
2 tablespoons salted butter, melted
½ tablespoon salt
2 cloves garlic, peeled and finely minced
50g grated Parmesan cheese, divided

1. Toss the cauliflower florets in a large bowl with the butter. Sprinkle with the salt, garlic, and 25g Parmesan. 2. Insert a crisper plate in a drawer, place the cauliflower florets in the drawer, and insert the drawer in the unit. 3. Select Zone 1 and turn the dial to select ROAST. Set the cooking temperature to 175°C and cook time to 15 minutes. Press the START/PAUSE button to begin cooking. Shake the drawer halfway through cooking. Cauliflower will be browned at the edges and tender when done. 4. Transfer the cauliflower florets to a large serving dish and sprinkle with the remaining Parmesan. Serve warm.

Bacon Wrapped Asparagus

⏱ **Prep Time:** 5 minutes   🍴 **Cook:** 10 minutes   🍂 **Serves:** 4

455g asparagus, trimmed (about 24 spears)
4 slices bacon or beef bacon
65g Dressing, for serving
2 tablespoons chopped fresh chives, for garnish

1. Insert a crisper plate in each drawer and spray the drawers with the avocado oil. 2. Slice the bacon down the middle, making long, thin strips. Wrap 1 slice of bacon around 3 asparagus spears and secure each end with a toothpick. Repeat with the remaining bacon and asparagus.
3. Place the asparagus bundles in the drawers in a single layer and insert the drawers in the unit. 4. Select Zone 1 and turn the dial to select AIR FRY. Set the cooking temperature to 200°C and cook time to 8 minutes. Press the MATCH COOK button to copy Zone 1's settings to Zone 2. Press START/PAUSE to begin cooking in both zones. Cook for 8 minutes for thin stalks, 10 minutes for medium to thick stalks, or until the asparagus is slightly charred on the ends and the bacon is crispy. 5. Serve with the ranch dressing or other sauce if desired, and garnish with chives. 6. Best served fresh. Store leftovers in an airtight container in the fridge for up to 5 days. Reheat in a preheated 200°C air fryer for 3 minutes, or until heated through.

Mac and Cheese

⏰ **Prep Time:** 10 minutes 🍲 **Cook:** 15 minutes 🍽 **Serves:** 4

360g frozen chopped cauliflower, thawed
55g cream cheese, softened
30g shredded Gruyère or Swiss cheese
30g shredded sharp cheddar cheese
2 tablespoons finely diced onions
3 tablespoons beef broth
¼ teaspoon fine sea salt
Topping:
10g pork dust
55g unsalted butter, melted, plus more for greasing ramekins
4 slices bacon, finely diced
For Garnish (Optional):
Chopped fresh thyme or chives

1. Place the cauliflower on a paper towel and pat dry. Cut any large pieces of cauliflower into ½-inch pieces. 2. In a medium-sized bowl, stir together the cream cheese, cheddar, Gruyère, and onions. Slowly stir in the broth and combine well. Add the salt and stir to combine. Add the cauliflower and stir gently to mix the cauliflower into the cheese sauce. 3. Grease four 115g ramekins with the butter. Divide the cauliflower mixture among the ramekins, filling each three-quarters full. 4. Make the topping by stirring together the pork dust, butter, and bacon in a small bowl until well combined. Divide the topping among the ramekins. 5. Insert the crisper plates in each drawer, place the ramekins in the drawers, and insert the drawers in the unit. 6. Select Zone 1 and turn the dial to select AIR FRY. Set the cooking temperature to 190°C and cook time to 15 minutes. Press the MATCH COOK button to copy Zone 1's settings to Zone 2. Press START/PAUSE to begin cooking in both zones. Cook until the topping is browned and the bacon is crispy. 7. Garnish with the fresh thyme or chives, if desired. 8. Store leftovers in the ramekins covered with foil. Reheat in a preheated 190°C air fryer for 6 minutes, or until the cauliflower is heated through and the top is crispy.

Spinach and Cheese Frittata

⏰ **Prep Time:** 10 minutes 🍲 **Cook:** 20 minutes 🍽 **Serves:** 4

6 large eggs
120g heavy whipping cream
190g frozen chopped spinach, drained
115g shredded sharp Cheddar cheese
30g peeled and diced yellow onion
½ teaspoon salt
¼ teaspoon ground black pepper

1. In a large bowl, whisk the eggs and cream together. Whisk in the spinach, onion, Cheddar, salt, and pepper. 2. Pour the mixture into an ungreased round nonstick baking dish that fits your air fryer. 3. Insert a crisper plate in a drawer, place the dish in the drawer, and insert the drawer in the unit. 4. Select Zone 1 and turn the dial to select BAKE. Set the cooking temperature to 160°C and cook time to 20 minutes. Press the START/PAUSE button to begin cooking. 5. Eggs will be firm and slightly browned when done. Serve immediately.

Easy Fluffy Pancake

⏰ Prep Time: 5 minutes 🍳 Cook: 30 minutes 🍃 Serves: 2

110g blanched finely ground almond flour
2 tablespoons granular erythritol
1 tablespoon salted butter, melted
1 large egg
80ml unsweetened almond milk
½ teaspoon vanilla extract

1. In a large bowl, mix all ingredients together, then pour half the batter into an ungreased round nonstick baking dish that fits your air fryer. 2. Insert a crisper plate in a drawer, place the dish in the drawer, and insert the drawer in the unit. 3. Select Zone 1 and turn the dial to select BAKE. Set the cooking temperature to 160°C and cook time to 15 minutes. Press the START/PAUSE button to begin cooking. 4. The pancake will be golden brown on top and firm, and a toothpick inserted in the centre will come out clean when done. Repeat with remaining batter. 5. Slice in half in dish and serve warm.

Courgette & Cauliflower Fritters

⏰ Prep Time: 15 minutes 🍳 Cook: 12 minutes 🍃 Serves: 2

1 (345g) cauliflower steamer bag
1 medium courgette, shredded
30g almond flour
1 large egg
½ teaspoon garlic powder
25g grated vegetarian Parmesan cheese

1. Cook the cauliflower according to the package instructions and drain excess moisture in cheesecloth or paper towel. Place into a large bowl. 2. Place the courgette into paper towel and pat down to remove excess moisture. Add to the bowl with cauliflower. Add the remaining ingredients. 3. Divide the mixture evenly and form four patties. Press into ¼"-thick patties. 4. Insert a crisper plate in a drawer, place the patties in the drawer, and insert the drawer in the unit. 5. Select Zone 1 and turn the dial to select AIR FRY. Set the cooking temperature to 160°C and cook time to 12 minutes. Press the START/PAUSE button to begin cooking. 6. Fritters will be firm when fully cooked. Allow to cool 5 minutes before moving. Serve warm.

Buttery Green Beans

⏰ **Prep Time: 5 minutes** 🍲 **Cook: 8-10 minutes** 🍽 **Serves: 6**

455g green beans, trimmed
1 tablespoon avocado oil
1 teaspoon garlic powder
Sea salt
Freshly ground black pepper
55g (4 tablespoons) unsalted butter, melted
25g freshly grated Parmesan cheese

1. In a large bowl, toss together the green beans, avocado oil, and garlic powder and season with the salt and pepper. 2. Place bottom layer of green beans in the drawer. Insert the Stacked Meal Rack and place the top layer of green beans on top. Insert the drawer in the unit. 3. Select DOUBLE STACK PRO. Select Zone 1, select ROAST, and set temperature to 230°C and time to 8 minutes. Press the START/PAUSE button to begin cooking. Cook for 8 to 10 minutes, tossing halfway through. 4. Transfer the green beans to a large bowl and toss with the melted butter. Top with the Parmesan cheese and serve warm.

Classic Aubergine Lasagna

⏰ **Prep Time: 10 minutes** 🍲 **Cook: 46 minutes** 🍽 **Serves: 4**

1 small aubergine (about 340g), sliced into rounds
2 teaspoons salt
1 tablespoon olive oil
115g shredded mozzarella, divided
250g ricotta cheese
1 large egg
25g grated Parmesan cheese
½ teaspoon dried oregano
375g no-sugar-added marinara
1 tablespoon chopped fresh parsley

1. Coat a casserole dish that fits your air fryer with the olive oil and set aside. 2. Arrange the aubergine slices in a single layer on a baking sheet and sprinkle with the salt. Let sit for 10 minutes. Use a paper towel to remove the excess moisture and salt. 3. Brush the aubergine with the olive oil. Place bottom layer of aubergine in the drawer. Insert the Stacked Meal Rack and place the top layer of aubergine on top. Insert the drawer in the unit. 4. Select DOUBLE STACK PRO. Select Zone 1, select AIR FRY, and set temperature to 175°C and time to 6 minutes. Press the START/PAUSE button to begin cooking. Cook until softened, pausing halfway through the cooking time to turn the aubergine. 5. Transfer the aubergine back to the baking sheet and let cool. 6. In a small bowl, combine 60g of the mozzarella with the ricotta, egg, Parmesan, and oregano. To assemble the lasagna, spread a spoonful of marinara in the bottom of the casserole dish, followed by a layer of aubergine, a layer of the cheese mixture, and a layer of marinara. Repeat the layers until all of the ingredients are used, ending with the remaining 55g of mozzarella. Scatter the parsley on top. Cover the baking dish with foil.
7. Place the dish in the drawer, increase the air fryer to 185°C, and air fry for 30 minutes. Uncover the dish and continue cooking for 10 minutes longer until the cheese begins to brown. 8. Allow the casserole to sit for at least 10 minutes before serving.

Crispy Fried Green Tomato Salad with Buttermilk Dressing

⏱ **Prep Time:** 10 minutes   🍲 **Cook:** 8-10 minutes   🥬 **Serves:** 4

4 green tomatoes
½ teaspoon salt
1 large egg, lightly beaten
30g peanut flour
1 tablespoon Creole seasoning
1 (140g) bag arugula

Buttermilk Dressing:
220g mayonnaise
115g sour cream
2 teaspoons fresh lemon juice
2 tablespoons finely chopped fresh parsley
1 teaspoon dried dill
1 teaspoon dried chives
½ teaspoon salt
½ teaspoon garlic powder
½ teaspoon onion powder

1. Slice the tomatoes into ½-inch slices and sprinkle with the salt. Let sit for 5 to 10 minutes. 2. Place the egg in a small shallow bowl. In another small shallow bowl, combine the peanut flour and Creole seasoning. Dip each tomato slice into the egg wash, then dip into the peanut flour mixture, turning to coat evenly. 3. Insert the crisper plates in each drawer, place the tomato slices in the drawers in a single layer, and spray both sides lightly with olive oil. Insert the drawers in the unit. 4. Select Zone 1 and turn the dial to select AIR FRY. Set the cooking temperature to 200°C and cook time to 8 minutes. Press the MATCH COOK button to copy Zone 1's settings to Zone 2. Press START/PAUSE to begin cooking in both zones. Air fry until browned and crisp, 8 to 10 minutes. 5. To make the buttermilk dressing by whisking together the mayonnaise, sour cream, dill, chives, salt, lemon juice, parsley, garlic powder, and onion powder in a small bowl. 6. Serve the tomato slices on top of a bed of the arugula with the dressing on the side.

Roasted Broccoli with Balsamic Sesame Dressing

⏱ **Prep Time:** 10 minutes   🍲 **Cook:** 10 minutes   🥬 **Serves:** 4

600g broccoli florets, cut into bite-size pieces
1 tablespoon olive oil
¼ teaspoon salt
2 tablespoons sesame seeds
2 tablespoons rice vinegar
2 tablespoons reduced-sodium soy sauce
2 tablespoons sesame oil
½ teaspoon Swerve sugar replacement
¼ teaspoon red pepper flakes (optional)

1. In a large bowl, toss the broccoli with the olive oil and salt until thoroughly coated. 2. Insert a crisper plate in a drawer, place the broccoli in the drawer, and insert the drawer in the unit. 3. Select Zone 1 and turn the dial to select ROAST. Set the cooking temperature to 200°C and cook time to 10 minutes. Press the START/PAUSE button to begin cooking. Cook until the stems are tender and the edges are beginning to crisp, pausing halfway through the cooking time to shake the drawer. 4. Meanwhile, in the same large bowl, whisk together the sesame seeds, vinegar, soy sauce, sesame oil, Swerve, and red pepper flakes (if using). 5. Transfer the broccoli to the bowl and toss until thoroughly coated with the seasonings. Serve warm or at room temperature.

Chapter 3 Snacks and Starters

Crispy Kale Chips

⏰ **Prep Time: 5 minutes** 🍲 **Cook: 10 minutes** 🍃 **Serves: 16**

½ teaspoon dried chives
½ teaspoon dried dill weed
½ teaspoon dried parsley
¼ teaspoon garlic powder
¼ teaspoon onion powder
⅛ teaspoon fine sea salt
⅛ teaspoon ground black pepper
2 large bunches kale

1. Insert a crisper plate in each drawer and spray the drawers with the avocado oil. 2. Place the seasonings, salt, and pepper in a small bowl and mix well. 3. Wash the kale and pat completely dry. Use a sharp knife to carve out the thick inner stems, then spray the leaves with avocado oil and sprinkle them with the seasoning mix. 4. Place the kale leaves in a single layer in the drawers and insert the drawers in the unit. 5. Select Zone 1 and turn the dial to select AIR FRY. Set the cooking temperature to 180°C and cook time to 10 minutes. Press the MATCH COOK button to copy Zone 1's settings to Zone 2. Press START/PAUSE to begin cooking in both zones. Shake and rotate the kale chips halfway through. 6. Transfer the chips to a baking sheet to cool completely and crisp up. Sprinkle the cooled chips with salt before serving, if desired. 7. Kale chips can be stored in an airtight container at room temperature for up to 1 week, but they are best eaten within 3 days

Savoury Ranch Chicken Bites

⏰ **Prep Time: 10 minutes** 🍲 **Cook: 15 minutes** 🍃 **Serves: 6**

2 (170g) boneless, skinless chicken breasts, cut into 1" cubes
1 tablespoon coconut oil
½ teaspoon salt
¼ teaspoon ground black pepper
40g ranch dressing
120g shredded Colby cheese
4 slices cooked sugar-free bacon, crumbled

1. Drizzle the chicken with the coconut oil. Sprinkle with the salt and pepper and place into an ungreased round nonstick baking dish that fits your air fryer. 2. Insert a crisper plate in a drawer, place the dish in the drawer, and insert the drawer in the unit. 3. Select Zone 1 and turn the dial to select AIR FRY. Set the cooking temperature to 185°C and cook time to 10 minutes. Press the START/PAUSE button to begin cooking. Stir the chicken halfway through cooking. 4. Drizzle the ranch dressing over the chicken and top with the Colby and bacon. Increase the temperature to 200°C and continue to cook for 5 minutes. 5. When done, chicken will be browned and have an internal temperature of at least 75°C. Serve warm.

Reuben Egg Rolls

⏱ **Prep Time:** 15 minutes   🍲 **Cook:** 10 minutes   🔖 **Serves:** 10

1 (230g) package cream cheese, softened
230g cooked corned beef, chopped
70g drained and chopped sauerkraut
55g shredded Swiss cheese
20 slices prosciutto
Thousand Island Dipping Sauce:
155g mayonnaise
60g chopped dill pickles
60g tomato sauce
2 tablespoons Swerve confectioners'-style sweetener or equivalent amount of liquid or powdered sweetener
⅛ teaspoon fine sea salt
Fresh thyme leaves, for garnish
Ground black pepper, for garnish
Sauerkraut, for serving (optional)

1. Insert a crisper plate in each drawer and spray the drawers with the avocado oil. 2. Make the filling by placing the cream cheese in a medium-sized bowl and stirring to break it up. Add the corned beef, sauerkraut, and Swiss cheese and stir well to combine. 3. Assemble the egg rolls. Lay 1 slice of prosciutto on a sushi mat or a sheet of parchment paper with a short end toward you. Lay another slice of prosciutto on top of it at a right angle, forming a cross. Spoon 3 to 4 tablespoons of the filling into the centre of the cross. 4. Fold the sides of the top slice up and over the filling to form the ends of the roll. Tightly roll up the long piece of prosciutto, starting at the edge closest to you, into a tight egg roll shape that overlaps by an inch or so. Repeat with the remaining prosciutto and filling. 5. Place the egg rolls in the drawer seam side down, leaving space between them, and insert the drawers in the unit. 6. Select Zone 1 and turn the dial to select AIR FRY. Set the cooking temperature to 200°C and cook time to 10 minutes. Press the MATCH COOK button to copy Zone 1's settings to Zone 2. Press START/PAUSE to begin cooking in both zones. Cook until the outside is crispy. 7. While the egg rolls are cooking, make the dipping sauce. In a small bowl, combine the mayo, pickles, sweetener, tomato sauce, and salt. Stir well and garnish with the thyme and ground black pepper. (The dipping sauce can be made up to 3 days ahead.) 8. Serve the egg rolls with the dipping sauce and sauerkraut if desired. 9. Best served fresh. Store leftovers in an airtight container in the refrigerator for up to 5 days or in the freezer for up to a month. Reheat in a preheated 200°C air fryer for 4 minutes, or until heated through and crispy.

Simple Cauliflower Tots

⏱ **Prep Time:** 10 minutes   🍲 **Cook:** 15 minutes   🔖 **Serves:** 6

325g cauliflower florets
1 tablespoon coconut flour
1 teaspoon fine sea salt
1 large egg, beaten
1 (230g) package cream cheese (or Kite Hill brand cream cheese style spread for dairy-free), softened
65g finely chopped onions
1 teaspoon smoked paprika
Chopped fresh parsley, for garnish (optional)
Ranch Dressing, for serving (optional)

1. Insert a crisper plate in each drawer and spray the drawers with the avocado oil. 2. Place the cauliflower in a food processor and pulse until it resembles grains of rice. 3. Place the riced cauliflower in a medium-sized bowl, sprinkle the coconut flour and salt on top, and toss well to coat. Add the egg, cream cheese, onions, and paprika and mix well to combine. 4. Form the cauliflower–cream cheese mixture into 24 tater tot shapes. 5. Place the tots in the drawer, leaving space between them, and insert the drawers in the unit. 6. Select Zone 1 and turn the dial to select AIR FRY. Set the cooking temperature to 200°C and cook time to 15 minutes. Press the MATCH COOK button to copy Zone 1's settings to Zone 2. Press START/PAUSE to begin cooking in both zones. Cook until golden brown. 7. Remove the tots from the air fryer and place them on a serving plate. Garnish with the chopped fresh parsley, if desired, and serve with the ranch dressing on the side for dipping, if desired. 8. Store leftovers in an airtight container in the fridge for 3 days or in the freezer for up to a month. Reheat in a preheated 200°C air fryer for 4 minutes, or until heated through.

Two-Ingredient Cheese Crisps

⏱ **Prep Time: 2 minutes** 🍲 **Cook: 10-12 minutes** 🍽 **Serves: 2**

55g shredded Cheddar cheese
1 egg white

1. Insert a crisper plate in each drawer and line the drawers with a piece of parchment paper. 2. In a medium bowl, stir together the cheese and egg white with a fork until thoroughly combined. 3. Place small scoops of the cheese mixture in a single layer in the drawers (about 1 inch apart). Use the fork to spread the mixture as thin as possible. Insert the drawer in the unit. 4. Select Zone 1 and turn the dial to select AIR FRY. Set the cooking temperature to 200°C and cook time to 10 minutes. Press the START/PAUSE button to begin cooking. Air fry for 10 to 12 minutes until the crisps are golden brown. 5. Let cool for a few minutes before transferring them to a plate. Store at room temperature in an airtight container for up to 3 days.

Savoury Tomatoes Provençal

⏱ **Prep Time: 10 minutes** 🍲 **Cook: 15 minutes** 🍽 **Serves: 4**

4 small ripe tomatoes connected on the vine
¼ teaspoon fine sea salt
¼ teaspoon ground black pepper
50g powdered Parmesan cheese
2 tablespoons chopped fresh parsley
25g minced onions
2 cloves garlic, minced
½ teaspoon chopped fresh thyme leaves
For Garnish:
Fresh parsley leaves
Ground black pepper
Sprig of fresh basil

1. Insert a crisper plate in a drawer and spray the drawer with the avocado oil. 2. Slice the tops off the tomatoes without removing them from the vine. Do not discard the tops. Use a large spoon to scoop the seeds out of the tomatoes. Sprinkle the insides of the tomatoes with the salt and pepper. 3. In a medium-sized bowl, combine the cheese, onions, parsley, garlic, and thyme. Stir to combine well. Divide the mixture evenly among the tomatoes. 4. Spray the avocado oil on the tomatoes. Place the tomato tops in the drawer next to, not on top of, the filled tomatoes. Insert the drawer in the unit. 5. Select Zone 1 and turn the dial to select ROAST. Set the cooking temperature to 175°C and cook time to 15 minutes. Press the START/PAUSE button to begin cooking. Cook until the filling is golden and the tomatoes are soft yet still holding their shape. 6. Garnish with the fresh parsley, ground black pepper, and a sprig of basil. Serve warm, with the tomato tops on the vine. 7. Store leftovers in an airtight container in the refrigerator for up to 4 days. Reheat in a preheated 175°C air fryer for about 3 minutes, until heated through.

Crispy Onion Rings

⏱ **Prep Time:** 15 minutes   🍳 **Cook:** 10 minutes   🍃 **Serves:** 6

1 large sweet onion
110g finely ground blanched almond flour
100g finely grated Parmesan cheese
1 tablespoon baking powder
1 teaspoon smoked paprika
Sea salt
Freshly ground black pepper
2 large eggs
1 tablespoon heavy (whipping) cream
Avocado oil spray

1. Cut the onion crosswise into ⅓-inch-thick rings. 2. In a medium bowl, combine the almond flour, Parmesan cheese, smoked paprika, baking powder, and salt and pepper to taste. 3. In a separate medium bowl, beat the eggs and heavy cream together. 4. Dip an onion ring in the egg mixture and then into the almond flour mixture. Press the almond flour mixture into the onion. Transfer to a parchment paper–lined baking sheet and repeat with the remaining onion slices. 5. Place bottom layer of onion rings in the drawer. Insert the Stacked Meal Rack and place the top layer of onion rings on top. Spray the onion rings with oil and insert the drawer in the unit. 6. Select DOUBLE STACK PRO. Select Zone 1, select AIR FRY, and set temperature to 175°C and time to 5 minutes. Press the START/PAUSE button to begin cooking. 7. Use a spatula to carefully reach under the onions and flip them. Spray the onion rings with oil again and cook for 5 minutes more. 8. When done, serve and enjoy.

Bacon-Wrapped Jalapeño Poppers

⏱ **Prep Time:** 15 minutes   🍳 **Cook:** 17-22 minutes   🍃 **Serves:** 12

12 jalapeño peppers
230g cream cheese, at room temperature
2 tablespoons minced onion
1 teaspoon garlic powder
½ teaspoon smoked paprika
Sea salt
Freshly ground black pepper
12 strips bacon

1. Cut the jalapeños in half lengthwise, then seed them and remove any remaining white membranes to make room for the filling. 2. Insert the crisper plates in each drawer, place the jalapeños in a single layer, cut-side down, in the drawers, and insert the drawers in the unit. 3. Select Zone 1 and turn the dial to select AIR FRY. Set the cooking temperature to 200°C and cook time to 7 minutes. Press the MATCH COOK button to copy Zone 1's settings to Zone 2. Press START/PAUSE to begin cooking in both zones. 4. Remove the jalapeños peppers from the air fryer and place them on a paper towel, cut-side up. Let them rest until they are cool enough to handle. 5. While the jalapeños peppers are cooking, in a medium bowl, stir together the garlic powder, cream cheese, minced onion, and smoked paprika. Season to taste with the salt and pepper. 6. Spoon the cream cheese filling into the jalapeños. 7. Slice the bacon strips in half, and wrap 1 piece of bacon around each stuffed jalapeño half. 8. Place the bacon-wrapped jalapeños cut-side up in the drawer in a single layer. Cook for 10 to 15 minutes, until the bacon is crispy. 9. When done, serve and enjoy.

Homemade French Fries

⏰ **Prep Time: 10 minutes** 🍲 **Cook: 25 minutes** 🍽 **Serves: 2-3**

2 to 3 russet potatoes, peeled and cut into ½-inch sticks
2 to 3 teaspoons olive or vegetable oil
Salt

1. Bring a large saucepan of salted water to a boil on the stovetop while you peel and cut the potatoes. Place the potatoes in the boiling salted water and blanch for 4 minutes. Strain the potatoes and rinse well with cold water. Pat dry them well with a clean kitchen towel.
2. Toss the dried potato sticks gently with the oil. Insert a crisper plate in a drawer, place the potato sticks in the drawer, and insert the drawer in the unit. 3. Select Zone 1 and turn the dial to select AIR FRY. Set the cooking temperature to 200°C and cook time to 25 minutes. Press the START/PAUSE button to begin cooking. Shake the drawer a few times while the fries cook to help them brown evenly and season the fries with the salt halfway through cooking. Serve them warm with the tomato ketchup, Sriracha mayonnaise or a mix of lemon zest, Parmesan cheese and parsley.

Parmesan-Rosemary Roasted Radishes

⏰ **Prep Time: 5 minutes** 🍲 **Cook: 15-20 minutes** 🍽 **Serves: 4**

1 bunch radishes, stemmed, trimmed, and quartered
1 tablespoon avocado oil
2 tablespoons finely grated fresh Parmesan cheese
1 tablespoon chopped fresh rosemary
Sea salt
Freshly ground black pepper

1. Place the radishes in a medium bowl and toss them with the avocado oil, Parmesan cheese, rosemary, salt, and pepper. 2. Place bottom layer of radishes in the drawer. Insert the Stacked Meal Rack and place the top layer of radishes on top. Insert the drawer in the unit. 3. Select DOUBLE STACK PRO. Select Zone 1, select ROAST, and set temperature to 190°C and time to 15 minutes. Press the START/PAUSE button to begin cooking. Cook for 15 to 20 minutes, until golden brown and tender. 4. Allow to cool for 5 minutes before serving.

Spinach and Artichoke Stuffed Mushrooms

⏲ **Prep Time:** 10 minutes 🍲 **Cook:** 10-14 minutes 🍽 **Serves:** 4

2 tablespoons olive oil
4 large Portobello mushrooms, stems removed and gills scraped out
½ teaspoon salt
¼ teaspoon freshly ground pepper
115g goat cheese, crumbled
130g chopped marinated artichoke hearts
190g frozen spinach, thawed and squeezed dry
50g grated Parmesan cheese
2 tablespoons chopped fresh parsley

1. Rub the olive oil over the Portobello mushrooms until thoroughly coated. Sprinkle both sides with the salt and black pepper. Place top-side down on a clean work surface. 2. In a small bowl, combine the goat cheese, artichoke hearts, and spinach. Mash with the back of a fork until thoroughly combined. Divide the cheese mixture among the mushrooms and sprinkle with the Parmesan cheese. 3. Insert a crisper plate in a drawer, place the mushrooms in the drawer, and insert the drawer in the unit. 4. Select Zone 1 and turn the dial to select AIR FRY. Set the cooking temperature to 200°C and cook time to 10 minutes. Press the START/PAUSE button to begin cooking. Air fry for 10 to 14 minutes until the mushrooms are tender and the cheese has begun to brown. 5. Top with the fresh parsley just before serving.

Crispy Spicy Tofu

⏲ **Prep Time:** 10 minutes 🍲 **Cook:** 15-20 minutes 🍽 **Serves:** 4

1 (455g) block extra-firm tofu
2 tablespoons reduced-sodium soy sauce
1 tablespoon toasted sesame oil
1 tablespoon olive oil
1 tablespoon chilli-garlic sauce
1½ teaspoons black sesame seeds
1 scallion, thinly sliced

1. Press the tofu for at least 15 minutes by wrapping it in paper towels and setting a heavy pan on top so that the moisture drains. 2. Slice the tofu into bite-size cubes and transfer to a bowl. Drizzle with the soy sauce, sesame oil, olive oil, and chilli-garlic sauce. Cover and refrigerate for 1 hour or up to overnight. 3. Place bottom layer of tofu in the drawer. Insert the Stacked Meal Rack and place the top layer of tofu on top. Insert the drawer in the unit. 4. Select DOUBLE STACK PRO. Select Zone 1, select AIR FRY, and set temperature to 200°C and time to 15 minutes. Press the START/PAUSE button to begin cooking. Air fry for 15 to 20 minutes until crisp, pausing to shake the drawer halfway through the cooking time. 5. Serve with any juices that accumulate in the bottom of the air fryer, sprinkled with the sesame seeds and sliced scallion.

Chapter 4 Poultry

Jalapeño Popper Hasselback Chicken

⏱ **Prep Time:** 20 minutes   🍲 **Cook:** 20 minutes   🥢 **Serves: 2**

4 slices sugar-free bacon, cooked and crumbled
55g full-fat cream cheese, softened
55g shredded sharp Cheddar cheese, divided
60g sliced pickled jalapeños
2 (170g) boneless, skinless chicken breasts

1. In a medium bowl, place cooked bacon, then fold in cream cheese, half of the Cheddar, and the jalapeño slices. 2. Use a sharp knife to make slits in each of the chicken breasts about ¾ of the way across the chicken, being careful not to cut all the way through. Depending on the size of the chicken breast, you'll likely have 6–8 slits per breast. 3. Spoon the cream cheese mixture into the slits of the chicken. Sprinkle remaining shredded cheese over chicken breasts. 4. Insert a crisper plate in a drawer, place the chicken breasts in the drawer, and insert the drawer in the unit. 5. Select Zone 1 and turn the dial to select AIR FRY. Set the cooking temperature to 175°C and cook time to 20 minutes. Press the START/PAUSE button to begin cooking. 6. Serve warm.

Classic Chicken Kiev

⏱ **Prep Time:** 15 minutes   🍲 **Cook:** 25 minutes   🥢 **Serves: 4**

225g (2 sticks) unsalted butter, softened (or butter-flavoured coconut oil for dairy-free)
2 tablespoons lemon juice
2 tablespoons plus 1 teaspoon chopped fresh parsley leaves, divided, plus more for garnish
2 tablespoons chopped fresh tarragon leaves
3 cloves garlic, minced
1 teaspoon fine sea salt, divided
4 (115g) boneless, skinless chicken breasts
2 large eggs
70g pork dust
1 teaspoon ground black pepper
Sprig of fresh parsley, for garnish
Lemon slices, for serving

1. Insert a crisper plate in each drawer and spray the drawers with the avocado oil. 2. In a medium-sized bowl, combine the butter, lemon juice, tarragon, garlic, 2 tablespoons of the parsley, and ¼ teaspoon of the salt. Cover and place in the fridge to harden for 7 minutes. 3. While the butter mixture chills, place one of the chicken breasts on a cutting board. With a sharp knife held parallel to the cutting board, make a 1-inch-wide incision at the top of the breast. Carefully cut into the breast to form a large pocket, leaving a ½-inch border along the sides and bottom. Repeat with the other 3 breasts. 4. Stuff one-quarter of the butter mixture into each chicken breast and secure the openings with toothpicks. 5. Beat the eggs in a small shallow dish. In another shallow dish, combine the pork dust, the remaining 1 teaspoon of parsley, the remaining ¾ teaspoon of salt, and the pepper. 6. One at a time, dip the chicken breasts in the egg, shake off the excess egg, and dredge the breasts in the pork dust mixture. Use your hands to press the pork dust onto each breast to form a nice crust. If you desire a thicker coating, dip it again in the egg and pork dust. As you finish, spray each coated chicken breast with avocado oil. 7. Place the chicken breasts in the drawers and insert the drawers in the unit. 8. Select Zone 1 and turn the dial to select AIR FRY. Set the cooking temperature to 175°C and cook time to 15 minutes. Press the MATCH COOK button to copy Zone 1's settings to Zone 2. Press START/PAUSE to begin cooking in both zones. 9. Flip the breasts and cook for another 10 minutes, or until the internal temperature of the chicken is 75°C and the crust is golden brown. 10. Serve garnished with the chopped fresh parsley and a parsley sprig, with lemon slices on the side. 11. Store leftovers in an airtight container in the refrigerator for up to 4 days or in the freezer for up to a month. Reheat in a preheated 175°C air fryer for 5 minutes, or until heated through.

Chicken Cordon Bleu Meatballs

⏰ Prep Time: 10 minutes   🍲 Cook: 15 minutes   🍃 Serves: 4

Meatballs:
230g ground chicken
230g ham, diced
55g finely grated Swiss cheese
30g chopped onions
3 cloves garlic, minced
1½ teaspoons fine sea salt
1 teaspoon ground black pepper, plus more for garnish if desired
1 large egg, beaten

Dijon Sauce:
60ml chicken broth, hot
3 tablespoons Dijon mustard
2 tablespoons lemon juice
¾ teaspoon fine sea salt
¼ teaspoon ground black pepper
Chopped fresh thyme leaves, for garnish (optional)

1. Insert a crisper plate in each drawer and spray the drawers with the avocado oil. 2. In a large bowl, mix all the ingredients for the meatballs with your hands until well combined. Shape the meat mixture into about twelve 1½-inch balls. 3. Place the meatballs in the drawers, leaving space between them, and insert the drawers in the unit. 4. Select Zone 1 and turn the dial to select AIR FRY. Set the cooking temperature to 200°C and cook time to 15 minutes. Press the MATCH COOK button to copy Zone 1's settings to Zone 2. Press START/PAUSE to begin cooking in both zones. Cook until cooked through and the internal temperature reaches 75°C. 5. While the meatballs cook, make the sauce by stirring together all the sauce ingredients in a small mixing bowl until well combined. 6. Pour the sauce into a serving dish and place the meatballs on top. Garnish with the ground black pepper and fresh thyme leaves, if desired. 7. Store leftover meatballs in an airtight container in the refrigerator for up to 5 days or in the freezer for up to a month. Reheat in a preheated 175°C air fryer for 4 minutes, or until heated through.

Thanksgiving Turkey Breast

⏰ Prep Time: 5 minutes   🍲 Cook: 30 minutes   🍃 Serves: 4

1½ teaspoons fine sea salt
1 teaspoon ground black pepper
1 teaspoon chopped fresh rosemary leaves
1 teaspoon chopped fresh sage
1 teaspoon chopped fresh tarragon
1 teaspoon chopped fresh thyme leaves
1 (910g) turkey breast
3 tablespoons ghee or unsalted butter, melted
3 tablespoons Dijon mustard

1. Insert a crisper plate in a drawer and spray the drawer with the avocado oil. 2. In a small bowl, stir together the salt, pepper, and herbs until well combined. Season the turkey breast generously on all sides with the seasoning. 3. In another small bowl, stir together the ghee and Dijon. Brush the ghee mixture on all sides of the turkey breast. 4. Place the turkey breast in the drawer and insert the drawer in the unit. 5. Select Zone 1 and turn the dial to select AIR FRY. Set the cooking temperature to 200°C and cook time to 30 minutes. Press the START/PAUSE button to begin cooking. Cook until the internal temperature reaches 75°C. 6. Transfer the breast to a cutting board and allow it to rest for 10 minutes before cutting it into ½-inch-thick slices. 7. Store leftovers in an airtight container in the refrigerator for up to 4 days or in the freezer for up to a month. Reheat in a preheated 175°C air fryer for 4 minutes, or until warmed through.

The Best Popcorn Chicken

⏰ **Prep Time:** 10 minutes 🍲 **Cook:** 15 minutes 📚 **Serves:** 4

110g mayonnaise
1 teaspoon prepared yellow mustard
55g finely shredded cheddar cheese
15g pork dust
¼ teaspoon garlic powder
¼ teaspoon onion powder
¼ teaspoon smoked paprika
455g boneless, skinless chicken breasts, cut into ½-inch pieces
Chopped fresh parsley, for garnish (optional)
Ranch Dressing, for serving (optional)

1. Insert a crisper plate in each drawer and spray the drawers with the avocado oil. 2. In a large bowl, mix together the mayonnaise and mustard. In a separate medium-sized bowl, mix together the cheese, garlic powder, onion powder, pork dust, and paprika until well combined. 3. Add the chicken pieces to the mayonnaise mixture and stir well to coat. One at a time, roll the coated chicken pieces in the pork dust mixture and spray them with avocado oil. 4. Place the chicken in the drawers, leaving space between them, and insert the drawers in the unit. 5. Select Zone 1 and turn the dial to select AIR FRY. Set the cooking temperature to 200°C and cook time to 12 minutes. Press the MATCH COOK button to copy Zone 1's settings to Zone 2. Press START/PAUSE to begin cooking in both zones. Cook the chicken for 12 to 15 minutes, until the internal temperature reaches 75°C and the coating is golden brown. 6. Garnish with the fresh parsley, if desired, and serve with the ranch dressing, if desired. 7. Store leftovers in an airtight container in the fridge for up to 4 days. Serve leftovers chilled or reheat in a preheated 200°C air fryer for 5 minutes, or until heated through.

Air-Fried Chicken Paillard

⏰ **Prep Time:** 10 minutes 🍲 **Cook:** 10 minutes 📚 **Serves:** 2

2 large eggs, room temperature
1 tablespoon water
50g powdered Parmesan cheese or pork dust
2 teaspoons dried thyme leaves
1 teaspoon ground black pepper
2 (140g) boneless, skinless chicken breasts, pounded to ½ inch thick
Lemon Butter Sauce:
2 tablespoons unsalted butter, melted
2 teaspoons lemon juice
¼ teaspoon finely chopped fresh thyme leaves, plus more for garnish
⅛ teaspoon fine sea salt
Lemon slices, for serving

1. Insert a crisper plate in a drawer and spray the drawer with the avocado oil. 2. Beat the eggs in a shallow dish, then add the water and stir well. 3. In a separate shallow dish, mix together the Parmesan, thyme, and pepper until well combined. 4. One at a time, dip the chicken breasts in the eggs and let any excess drip off, then dredge both sides of the chicken in the Parmesan mixture. 5. Place the coated chicken in the drawer and insert the drawer in the unit. 6. Select Zone 1 and turn the dial to select AIR FRY. Set the cooking temperature to 200°C and cook time to 5 minutes. Press the START/PAUSE button to begin cooking. 7. Flip the chicken and cook for another 5 minutes, or until cooked through and the internal temperature reaches 75°C . 8. While the chicken cooks, make the lemon butter sauce by stirring together all the sauce ingredients in a small bowl until well combined. 9. Place the chicken on a plate and pour the sauce over it. Garnish with the chopped fresh thyme and serve with lemon slices. 10. Store leftovers in an airtight container in the refrigerator for up to 4 days. Reheat in a preheated 200°C air fryer for 5 minutes, or until heated through.

Lemon Pepper Drumsticks

⏱ **Prep Time:** 5 minutes   🍳 **Cook:** 25 minutes   🍽 **Serves:** 4

2 teaspoons baking powder
½ teaspoon garlic powder
8 chicken drumsticks
4 tablespoons salted butter, melted
1 tablespoon lemon pepper seasoning

1. Sprinkle the baking powder and garlic powder over the drumsticks and rub into the chicken skin. 2. Insert the crisper plates in each drawer, place the drumsticks in the drawers, and insert the drawers in the unit. 3. Select Zone 1 and turn the dial to select AIR FRY. Set the cooking temperature to 190°C and cook time to 25 minutes. Press the MATCH COOK button to copy Zone 1's settings to Zone 2. Press START/PAUSE to begin cooking in both zones. 4. Use tongs to turn the drumsticks halfway through the cooking time. 5. When skin is golden and internal temperature is at least 75°C, remove the drumsticks from the air fryer. 6. In a large bowl, mix the butter and lemon pepper seasoning. Add the drumsticks to the bowl and toss until coated. Serve warm.

Chicken Strips with Satay Sauce

⏱ **Prep Time:** 5 minutes   🍳 **Cook:** 10 minutes   🍽 **Serves:** 4

4 (170g) boneless, skinless chicken breasts, sliced into 16 (1-inch) strips
1 teaspoon fine sea salt
1 teaspoon paprika
Sauce:
60g creamy almond butter (or sunflower seed butter for nut-free)
2 tablespoons chicken broth
1½ tablespoons coconut vinegar or unseasoned rice vinegar
1 clove garlic, minced
1 teaspoon peeled and minced fresh ginger
½ teaspoon hot sauce
⅛ teaspoon stevia glycerite, or 2 to 3 drops liquid stevia
For Garnish/Serving (Optional):
5g chopped cilantro leaves
Red pepper flakes
Sea salt flakes
Thinly sliced red, orange, and yellow bell peppers
Special Equipment:
16 wooden or bamboo skewers, soaked in water for 15 minutes

1. Insert a crisper plate in each drawer and spray the drawers with the avocado oil. 2. Thread the chicken strips onto the skewers. Season on all sides with the salt and paprika. 3. Place the chicken skewers in the drawers and insert the drawers in the unit. 4. Select Zone 1 and turn the dial to select AIR FRY. Set the cooking temperature to 200°C and cook time to 5 minutes. Press the MATCH COOK button to copy Zone 1's settings to Zone 2. Press START/PAUSE to begin cooking in both zones. 5. Flip and cook for another 5 minutes, until the chicken is cooked through and the internal temperature reaches 75°C. 6. While the chicken skewers cook, make the sauce by stirring together all the sauce ingredients in a medium-sized bowl until well combined. Taste and adjust the sweetness and heat to your liking. 7. Remove the chicken strips from the skewers, if desired. Garnish the chicken with cilantro, red pepper flakes, and salt flakes, if desired, and serve with the sliced bell peppers, if desired. Serve the sauce on the side. 8. Store leftovers in an airtight container in the fridge for up to 4 days or in the freezer for up to a month. Reheat in a preheated 175°C air fryer for 3 minutes per side, or until heated through.

Chicken Pesto Parmigiana

⏱ **Prep Time:** 10 minutes   🍲 **Cook:** 23 minutes   🍴 **Serves:** 4

2 large eggs
1 tablespoon water
Fine sea salt and ground black pepper
100g powdered Parmesan cheese
2 teaspoons Italian seasoning
4 (140g) boneless, skinless chicken breasts or thighs, pounded to ¼ inch thick
250g pesto
115g shredded mozzarella cheese
Finely chopped fresh basil, for garnish (optional)
Grape tomatoes, halved, for serving (optional)

1. Insert a crisper plate in each drawer and spray the drawers with the avocado oil. 2. Crack the eggs into a shallow baking dish, add the water and a pinch each of salt and pepper, and whisk to combine. In another shallow baking dish, mix together the Parmesan and Italian seasoning until well combined. 3. Season the chicken breasts well on both sides with the salt and pepper. Dip one chicken breast in the eggs and let any excess drip off, then dredge both sides of the breast in the Parmesan mixture. Spray the chicken breast with avocado oil. Repeat with the remaining 3 chicken breasts. 4. Place the chicken breasts in the drawers and insert the drawers in the unit. 5. Select Zone 1 and turn the dial to select AIR FRY. Set the cooking temperature to 200°C and cook time to 20 minutes. Press the MATCH COOK button to copy Zone 1's settings to Zone 2. Press START/PAUSE to begin cooking in both zones. Cook the chicken until the internal temperature reaches 75°C and the breading is golden brown, flipping halfway through. 6. Dollop each chicken breast with 60g of the pesto and top with the mozzarella. Return the breasts to the air fryer and cook for 3 minutes, or until the cheese is melted. Garnish with the basil and serve with the halved grape tomatoes on the side, if desired. 7. Store leftovers in an airtight container in the refrigerator for up to 4 days. Reheat in a preheated 200°C air fryer for 5 minutes, or until warmed through.

Garlic Parmesan Turkey Meatballs

⏱ **Prep Time:** 10 minutes   🍲 **Cook:** 7-10 minutes   🍴 **Serves:** 4

1 red bell pepper, seeded and coarsely chopped
2 cloves garlic, coarsely chopped
5g chopped fresh parsley
680g 85% lean ground turkey
1 egg, lightly beaten
50g grated Parmesan cheese
1 teaspoon salt
½ teaspoon freshly ground black pepper

1. In a food processor fitted with a metal blade, combine the bell pepper, garlic, and parsley. Pulse until finely chopped. Transfer the vegetables to a large mixing bowl. 2. Add the turkey, egg, Parmesan, salt, and black pepper. Mix gently until thoroughly combined. Shape the mixture into 1¼-inch meatballs. 3. Insert the crisper plates in each drawer, place the meatballs in a single layer in the drawers, and coat lightly with olive oil spray. Insert the drawers in the unit. 4. Select Zone 1 and turn the dial to select AIR FRY. Set the cooking temperature to 200°C and cook time to 7 minutes. Press the MATCH COOK button to copy Zone 1's settings to Zone 2. Press START/PAUSE to begin cooking in both zones. Air fry for 7 to 10 minutes, until lightly browned and a thermometer inserted into the centre of a meatball registers 75°C, pausing halfway through the cooking time to shake the drawer. 5. When done, serve and enjoy.

Blackened Chicken Tenders

⏰ **Prep Time:** 10 minutes 🍲 **Cook:** 17 minutes 🍃 **Serves:** 4

2 teaspoons paprika
1 teaspoon chilli powder
½ teaspoon garlic powder
½ teaspoon dried thyme
¼ teaspoon onion powder
⅛ teaspoon ground cayenne pepper
2 tablespoons coconut oil
455g boneless, skinless chicken tenders
30g full-fat ranch dressing

1. In a small bowl, combine all seasonings. 2. Drizzle oil over the chicken tenders and then generously coat each tender in the spice mixture. 3. Insert a crisper plate in a drawer, place the chicken tenders in the drawer, and insert the drawer in the unit. 4. Select Zone 1 and turn the dial to select AIR FRY. Set the cooking temperature to 190°C and cook time to 17 minutes. Press the START/PAUSE button to begin cooking. 5. Tenders will be 75°C internally when fully cooked. Serve with the ranch dressing for dipping.

Tandoori Chicken Thighs

⏰ **Prep Time:** 10 minutes 🍲 **Cook:** 15-20 minutes 🍃 **Serves:** 6

60g plain Greek yoghurt
2 cloves garlic, minced
1 tablespoon grated fresh ginger
½ teaspoon ground cayenne
½ teaspoon ground turmeric
½ teaspoon garam masala
1 teaspoon ground cumin
1 teaspoon salt
910g boneless chicken thighs, skin on
2 tablespoons chopped fresh cilantro
1 lemon, cut into 6 wedges
½ sweet onion, sliced

1. In a small bowl, combine the yoghurt, garlic, turmeric, garam masala, ginger, cayenne, cumin, and salt. Whisk until thoroughly combined. 2. Transfer the yoghurt mixture to a large resealable bag. Add the chicken, seal the bag, and massage the bag to ensure chicken is evenly coated. Refrigerate for 1 hour (or up to 8 hours). 3. Insert the crisper plates in each drawer. Remove the chicken from the marinade (discard the marinade) and arrange in a single layer in the drawers. Insert the drawers in the unit. 4. Select Zone 1 and turn the dial to select AIR FRY. Set the cooking temperature to 180°C and cook time to 15 minutes. Press the MATCH COOK button to copy Zone 1's settings to Zone 2. Press START/PAUSE to begin cooking in both zones. Air fry for 15 to 20 minutes, until a thermometer inserted into the thickest part registers 75°C, pausing halfway through the cooking time to flip the chicken. 5. Transfer the chicken to a serving platter. Top with the cilantro and serve with the lemon wedges and sliced onion.

Chicken Cordon Bleu

⏰ **Prep Time:** 15 minutes 🍲 **Cook:** 25 minutes ◈ **Serves:** 4

2 (225g) boneless, skinless chicken breasts
8 thin slices deli ham
4 slices Swiss cheese
½ teaspoon black pepper
1 large egg
80g panko bread crumbs or crushed pork rinds
Vegetable oil spray

1. Cut the chicken breasts horizontally in half to create four thin chicken cutlets. Place two slices of ham and one slice of cheese on each piece of chicken. Sprinkle with the pepper. Starting on a short end, roll up each piece of chicken and secure with a toothpick. 2. In a shallow bowl, beat the egg. Place the bread crumbs on a plate. Dip each chicken roll in the egg, then roll in the bread crumbs to coat. Spray all sides generously with vegetable oil spray. 3. Insert a crisper plate in a drawer, place the chicken in the drawer, and insert the drawer in the unit. 4. Select Zone 1 and turn the dial to select AIR FRY. Set the cooking temperature to 175°C and cook time to 25 minutes. Press the START/PAUSE button to begin cooking. 5. Turn the chicken and spray with oil spray halfway through the cooking time. Use a meat thermometer to ensure the chicken has reached an internal temperature of 75°C. 6. When done, serve and enjoy.

Crispy Indonesian Chicken Wings

⏰ **Prep Time:** 10 minutes 🍲 **Cook:** 25 minutes ◈ **Serves:** 2-3

For the Sauce:
75g kecap manis
2 tablespoons sambal oelek chilli sauce
2 tablespoons Worcestershire sauce
Chopped fresh cilantro, for garnish
For the Chicken:
455g chicken wings
1 tablespoon vegetable oil
½ teaspoon kosher salt
¼ teaspoon black pepper

To make the sauce: 1. In a small bowl stir together the kecap manis, sambal oelek, and Worcestershire sauce.
To make the chicken: 1. In a large bowl, drizzle the chicken with the oil, sprinkle with the salt and pepper, and toss to coat. 2. Insert a crisper plate in a drawer, place the wings in the drawer, and insert the drawer in the unit. 3. Select Zone 1 and turn the dial to select AIR FRY. Set the cooking temperature to 200°C and cook time to 20 minutes. Press the START/PAUSE button to begin cooking. Turn once halfway through the cooking time. 4. Transfer the wings to a clean, large bowl. Drizzle with about half of the sauce and toss to coat. Return the wings to the air fryer. Continue to cook for 5 minutes more, or until the wings' skin is browned and crisp. 5. Return the wings to the bowl and drizzle with the remaining sauce. Toss to coat. Transfer the wings to a serving platter and sprinkle with the cilantro.

Chapter 5 Beef, Pork, and Lamb

Healthy Carne Asada

⏰ **Prep Time:** 5 minutes   🍲 **Cook:** 8 minutes   🥩 **Serves:** 4

455g skirt steak, cut into 4 equal portions
Marinade:
15g fresh cilantro leaves and stems, plus more for garnish if desired
1 jalapeño pepper, seeded and diced
120ml lime juice
2 tablespoons avocado oil
2 tablespoons coconut vinegar or apple cider vinegar
2 teaspoons orange extract
1 teaspoon stevia glycerite, or ⅛ teaspoon liquid stevia
2 teaspoons ancho chilli powder
2 teaspoons fine sea salt
1 teaspoon coriander seeds
1 teaspoon cumin seeds
For Serving (Optional):
Chopped avocado
Lime slices
Sliced radishes

1. Place all the ingredients for the marinade in a blender and puree until smooth. 2. Put the steak in a shallow dish and pour the marinade over it, making sure the meat is covered completely. Cover and place in the fridge for 2 hours or overnight. 3. Remove the steak from the marinade. Place bottom layer of steak in the drawer sprayed with the avocado oil. Insert the Stacked Meal Rack sprayed with the avocado oil and place the top layer of steak on top. Insert the drawer in the unit. 4. Select DOUBLE STACK PRO. Select Zone 1, select ROAST, and set temperature to 200°C and time to 8 minutes. Press the START/PAUSE button to begin cooking. Cook until the internal temperature is 60°C; do not overcook or it will become tough. 5. Remove the steak from the air fryer and place it on a cutting board to rest for 10 minutes before slicing it against the grain. Garnish with the cilantro, if desired, and serve with the chopped avocado, lime slices, and/or sliced radishes, if desired. 6. Store leftovers in an airtight container in the fridge for 3 days or in the freezer for up to a month. Reheat in a preheated 175°C air fryer for 4 minutes, or until heated through.

Salisbury Steak with Mushroom Onion Gravy

⏰ **Prep Time:** 10 minutes   🍲 **Cook:** 33 minutes   🥩 **Serves:** 2

Mushroom Onion Gravy:
160g sliced button mushrooms
30g thinly sliced onions
55g unsalted butter, melted (or bacon fat for dairy-free)
½ teaspoon fine sea salt
60ml beef broth
Steaks:
230g ground beef (85% lean)
25g minced onions, or ½ teaspoon onion powder
2 tablespoons tomato paste
1 tablespoon dry mustard
1 clove garlic, minced, or ¼ teaspoon garlic powder
½ teaspoon fine sea salt
¼ teaspoon ground black pepper, plus more for garnish if desired
Chopped fresh thyme leaves, for garnish (optional)

To make the gravy: 1. Place the mushrooms and onions in a casserole dish that will fit your air fryer. Pour the melted butter over them and stir to coat, then season with the salt. 2. Insert a crisper plate in a drawer, place the dish in the drawer, and insert the drawer in the unit. 3. Select Zone 1 and turn the dial to select ROAST. Set the cooking temperature to 200°C and cook time to 5 minutes. Press the START/PAUSE button to begin cooking. 4. Stir, then cook for another 3 minutes, or until the onions are soft and the mushrooms are browning. Add the broth and cook for another 10 minutes.
To make the steaks: 1. While the gravy is cooking, prepare the steaks. In a large bowl, mix together the ground beef, tomato paste, onions, dry mustard, garlic, salt, and pepper until well combined. Form the mixture into 2 oval-shaped patties. 2. Place the patties on top of the mushroom gravy. Cook for 10 minutes, gently flip the patties, then cook for another 2 to 5 minutes, until the beef is cooked through and the internal temperature reaches 60°C. 3. Transfer the steaks to a serving platter and pour the gravy over them. Garnish with the ground black pepper and chopped fresh thyme, if desired. 4. Store leftovers in an airtight container in the fridge for 3 days or in the freezer for up to a month. Reheat in a preheated 175°C air fryer for 4 minutes, or until heated through.

Cheeseburger Meatballs

⏰ Prep Time: 10 minutes   🍳 Cook: 16 minutes   🍲 Serves: 4

455g ground beef
30g diced onions
1 large egg
1½ teaspoons smoked paprika
½ teaspoon fine sea salt
½ teaspoon garlic powder
½ teaspoon ground black pepper
230g mushrooms, finely chopped
120g tomato sauce
1 dozen (½-inch) cubes cheddar cheese
For Serving (Optional):
Prepared yellow mustard
Sugar-free or reduced-sugar ketchup

1. Insert a crisper plate in each drawer and spray the drawers with the avocado oil. 2. In a large bowl, mix together the ground beef, paprika, salt, garlic powder, onions, egg, and pepper until well combined. Add the mushrooms and slowly stir in the tomato sauce. The meat mixture should be very moist but still retain its shape when rolled into meatballs. 3. Divide the meat mixture into 12 equal portions. Place 1 cube of cheese in the centre of each portion and form the meat around the cheese into a 2-inch meatball. 4. Place the meatballs in a single layer in the drawers, leaving space between them, and insert the drawers in the unit. 5. Select Zone 1 and turn the dial to select AIR FRY. Set the cooking temperature to 190°C and cook time to 8 minutes. Press the MATCH COOK button to copy Zone 1's settings to Zone 2. Press START/PAUSE to begin cooking in both zones. 6. Flip them over and lower the temperature to 160°C. Cook for an additional 6 to 8 minutes, until cooked through. 7. Serve with the mustard and ketchup, if desired. 8. Store leftovers in an airtight container in the refrigerator for up to 4 days or in the freezer for up to 2 months. Reheat in a preheated 175°C air fryer for about 3 minutes, until heated through.

Herbed Lamb Chops

⏰ Prep Time: 10 minutes   🍳 Cook: 5 minutes   🍲 Serves: 2

1 large egg
2 cloves garlic, minced
10g pork dust
25g powdered Parmesan cheese (or pork dust for dairy-free)
1 tablespoon chopped fresh oregano leaves
1 tablespoon chopped fresh rosemary leaves
1 teaspoon chopped fresh thyme leaves
½ teaspoon ground black pepper
4 (1-inch-thick) lamb chops
For Garnish/Serving (Optional):
Sprigs of fresh oregano
Sprigs of fresh rosemary
Sprigs of fresh thyme
Lavender flowers
Lemon slices

1. Insert a crisper plate in each drawer and spray the drawers with the avocado oil. 2. Beat the egg in a shallow bowl, add the garlic, and stir well to combine. In another shallow bowl, mix together the pork dust, Parmesan, herbs, and pepper. 3. One at a time, dip the lamb chops into the egg mixture, shake off the excess egg, and then dredge them in the Parmesan mixture. Use your hands to coat the chops well in the Parmesan mixture and form a nice crust on all sides; if necessary, dip the chops again in both the egg and the Parmesan mixture. 4. Place the lamb chops in the drawer, leaving space between them, and insert the drawers in the unit. 5. Select Zone 1 and turn the dial to select AIR FRY. Set the cooking temperature to 200°C and cook time to 5 minutes. Press the MATCH COOK button to copy Zone 1's settings to Zone 2. Press START/PAUSE to begin cooking in both zones. Cook until the internal temperature reaches 60°C for medium doneness. 6. Let rest for 10 minutes before serving. Garnish with sprigs of oregano, rosemary, and thyme, and lavender flowers, if desired. Serve with lemon slices, if desired. 7. Best served fresh. Store leftovers in an airtight container in the fridge for up to 4 days. Serve chilled over a salad, or reheat in a 175°C air fryer for 3 minutes, or until heated through.

Zesty Black and Blue Burgers

⏱ **Prep Time: 5 minutes** 🍲 **Cook: 10 minutes** 🍽 **Serves: 2**

½ teaspoon fine sea salt
¼ teaspoon ground black pepper
¼ teaspoon garlic powder
¼ teaspoon onion powder
¼ teaspoon smoked paprika
2 (115g) hamburger patties, ½ inch thick
55g crumbled blue cheese (omit for dairy-free)
2 Hamburger Buns
2 tablespoons mayonnaise
6 red onion slices
2 Boston lettuce leaves

1. Insert a crisper plate in a drawer and spray the drawer with the avocado oil. 2. In a small bowl, combine the salt, pepper, and seasonings. Season the patties well on both sides with the seasoning mixture. 3. Insert a crisper plate in a drawer, place the patties in the drawer, and insert the drawer in the unit. 4. Select Zone 1 and turn the dial to select ROAST. Set the cooking temperature to 180°C and cook time to 7 minutes. Press the START/PAUSE button to begin cooking. Cook until the internal temperature reaches 60°C for a medium-done burger. 5. Place the blue cheese on top of the patties and cook for another minute to melt the cheese. Remove the burgers from the air fryer and allow to rest for 5 minutes. 6. Slice the buns in half and smear 2 halves with a tablespoon of mayo each. Increase the heat to 200°C and place the buns in the drawer cut side up. Cook the buns for 1 to 2 minutes, until golden brown. 7. Remove the buns from the air fryer and place them on a serving plate. Place the burgers on the buns and top each burger with 3 red onion slices and a lettuce leaf. 8. Best served fresh. Store leftover patties in an airtight container in the fridge for 3 days or in the freezer for up to a month. Reheat in a preheated 175°C air fryer for 4 minutes, or until heated through.

Pork Kebabs with Bell Peppers and Onions

⏱ **Prep Time: 15 minutes** 🍲 **Cook: 6-8 minutes** 🍽 **Serves: 4**

60ml coconut aminos
70g sugar-free ketchup
2 tablespoons freshly squeezed lime juice
2 tablespoons brown sugar substitute, such as Swerve or Sukrin Gold
1 teaspoon minced garlic
Sea salt
Freshly ground black pepper
240ml stevia-sweetened ginger ale, such as Zevia brand (optional)
455g pork tenderloin, cut into 1½-inch cubes
1 red bell pepper, cut into 1½-inch pieces
1 small red onion, cut into 1½-inch pieces

1. In a small bowl, whisk together the coconut aminos, brown sugar substitute, garlic, ketchup, lime juice, and salt and pepper to taste. Whisk in the ginger ale (if using). 2. Place the pork in a shallow dish and pour the marinade over top. Cover the dish with plastic wrap and let the pork marinate in the refrigerator for 2 to 4 hours. 3. Thread the marinated pork cubes, red bell pepper, and onion on skewers, alternating as you go. 4. Insert the crisper plates in each drawer, place the kebabs in the drawers in a single layer, and insert the drawers in the unit. 5. Select Zone 1 and turn the dial to select AIR FRY. Set the cooking temperature to 190°C and cook time to 6 minutes. Press the MATCH COOK button to copy Zone 1's settings to Zone 2. Press START/PAUSE to begin cooking in both zones. Cook for 6 to 8 minutes, until an instant-read thermometer reads 60°C. 6. When done, serve and enjoy.

Italian Sausages with Peppers and Onions

⏰ **Prep Time:** 5 minutes 🍴 **Cook:** 28 minutes 🥩 **Serves:** 3

1 medium onion, thinly sliced
1 yellow or orange bell pepper, thinly sliced
1 red bell pepper, thinly sliced
60ml avocado oil or melted coconut oil
1 teaspoon fine sea salt
6 Italian sausages
Dijon mustard, for serving (optional)

1. Place the onion and peppers in a large bowl. Drizzle with the oil and toss well to coat the veggies. Season with the salt. 2. Place the onion and peppers in a pie pan that fits your air fryer. 3. Insert a crisper plate in a drawer, place the pie pan in the drawer, and insert the drawer in the unit. 4. Select Zone 1 and turn the dial to select ROAST. Set the cooking temperature to 200°C and cook time to 8 minutes. Press the START/PAUSE button to begin cooking. Stir halfway through. 4. Remove the pie pan from the air fryer and set aside. 5. Spray the drawer with avocado oil, place the sausages in the drawer, and cook for 20 minutes, or until crispy and golden brown. 6. During the last minute or two of cooking, add the onion and peppers to the drawer with the sausages to warm them through. 7. Place the onion and peppers on a serving platter and arrange the sausages on top. Serve the Dijon mustard on the side, if desired. 8. Store leftovers in an airtight container in the fridge for up to 7 days or in the freezer for up to a month. Reheat in a preheated 200°C air fryer for 3 minutes, or until heated through.

Chinese Five-Spice Pork Belly

⏰ **Prep Time:** 10 minutes 🍴 **Cook:** 17 minutes 🥩 **Serves:** 4

455g unsalted pork belly
2 teaspoons Chinese five-spice powder
Sauce:
1 tablespoon coconut oil
1 (1-inch) piece fresh ginger, peeled and grated
2 cloves garlic, minced
120ml beef or chicken broth
30g to 60g Swerve confectioners'-style sweetener or equivalent amount of liquid or powdered sweetener
3 tablespoons wheat-free tamari, or 120ml coconut aminos
1 green onion, sliced, plus more for garnish
1 drop orange oil, or ½ teaspoon orange extract (optional)

1. Cut the pork belly into ½-inch-thick slices and season well on all sides with the five-spice powder. 2. Place bottom layer of pork belly in the drawer sprayed with the avocado oil. Insert the Stacked Meal Rack sprayed with the avocado oil and place the top layer of pork belly on top. Insert the drawer in the unit. 3. Select DOUBLE STACK PRO. Select Zone 1, select AIR FRY, and set temperature to 200°C and time to 8 minutes. Press the START/PAUSE button to begin cooking. Cook until cooked to your liking, flipping halfway through. 4. While the pork belly cooks, make the sauce. In a small saucepan over medium heat, heat the coconut oil. Add the ginger and garlic and sauté for 1 minute, or until fragrant. Add the broth, sweetener, and tamari and simmer for 10 to 15 minutes, until thickened. Add the green onion and cook for another minute, until the green onion is softened. Add the orange oil (if using). Taste and adjust the seasoning to your liking. 5. Transfer the pork belly to a large bowl. Pour the sauce over the pork belly and coat well. Place the pork belly slices on a serving platter and garnish with the sliced green onions. 6. Best served fresh. Store leftovers in an airtight container in the fridge for up to 4 days. Reheat in a preheated 200°C air fryer for 3 minutes, or until heated through.

Ground Beef Taco Rolls

⏱ **Prep Time: 20 minutes** 🍲 **Cook: 10 minutes** ❧ **Serves: 4**

230g 80/20 ground beef
80ml water
1 tablespoon chilli powder
2 teaspoons cumin
½ teaspoon garlic powder
¼ teaspoon dried oregano
60g canned diced tomatoes and chillies, drained
2 tablespoons chopped cilantro
175g shredded mozzarella cheese
55g blanched finely ground almond flour
55g full-fat cream cheese
1 large egg

1. In a medium skillet over medium heat, brown the ground beef for about 7–10 minutes. When meat is fully cooked, drain. 2. Add the water to the skillet and stir in the chilli powder, cumin, oregano, garlic powder, and tomatoes with chillies. Add the cilantro. Bring to a boil, then reduce the heat to simmer for 3 minutes. 3. In a large microwave-safe bowl, place the mozzarella, cream cheese, almond flour, and egg. Microwave for 1 minute. Stir the mixture quickly until smooth ball of dough forms. 4. Cut a piece of parchment for your work surface. Press the dough into a large rectangle on the parchment, wetting your hands to prevent the dough from sticking as necessary. Cut the dough into eight rectangles. 5. On each rectangle, place a few spoons of the meat mixture. Fold the short ends of each roll toward the centre and roll the length as you would a burrito. 6. Cut a piece of parchment to fit your air fryer drawer. Place taco rolls onto the parchment. 7. Insert a crisper plate in a drawer, place the parchment in the drawer, and insert the drawer in the unit. 8. Select Zone 1 and turn the dial to select AIR FRY. Set the cooking temperature to 180°C and cook time to 10 minutes. Press the START/PAUSE button to begin cooking. Flip halfway through the cooking time. 9. Allow to cool 10 minutes before serving.

Parmesan-Crusted Steak

⏱ **Prep Time: 10 minutes** 🍲 **Cook: 12 minutes** ❧ **Serves: 6**

115g (1 stick) unsalted butter, at room temperature
100g finely grated Parmesan cheese
30g finely ground blanched almond flour
680g New York strip steak
Sea salt
Freshly ground black pepper

1. Place the butter, Parmesan cheese, and almond flour in a food processor. Process until smooth. Transfer to a sheet of parchment paper and form into a log. Wrap tightly in plastic wrap. Freeze for 45 minutes or refrigerate for at least 4 hours. 2. While the butter is chilling, season the steak liberally with the salt and pepper. Let the steak rest at room temperature for about 45 minutes. 3. Insert the crisper plates in each drawer, place the steak in the drawers, and insert the drawers in the unit. 4. Select Zone 1 and turn the dial to select AIR FRY. Set the cooking temperature to 200°C and cook time to 4 minutes. Press the MATCH COOK button to copy Zone 1's settings to Zone 2. Press START/PAUSE to begin cooking in both zones. 5. Flip and cook for 3 minutes more, until the steak is brown on both sides. 6. Remove the steak from the air fryer and arrange an equal amount of the Parmesan butter on top of each steak. Return the steak to the air fryer and continue cooking for another 5 minutes, until an instant-read thermometer reads 50°C for medium-rare and the crust is golden brown (or to your desired doneness). 7. Transfer the cooked steak to a plate and let rest for 10 minutes before serving.

Crispy Pork Chops

⏰ **Prep Time: 10 minutes** 🍲 **Cook: 12-15 minutes** 🍽 **Serves: 4**

4 thick centre-cut pork chops (about 680g) (boneless best)
240ml buttermilk
40g crushed pork rinds
25g grated Parmesan cheese
1 teaspoon smoked paprika
½ teaspoon onion powder
½ teaspoon chilli powder
1 large egg
½ teaspoon salt
¼ teaspoon freshly ground black pepper

1. In a gallon-size resealable bag, combine the pork chops and buttermilk. Seal the bag and massage the meat to coat with the buttermilk. Refrigerate for at least 2 hours, preferably overnight. 2. In a shallow bowl, combine the pork rinds, paprika, onion powder, Parmesan, and chilli powder. In a separate shallow bowl, lightly beat the egg. 3. Remove the pork chops from the buttermilk marinade (discard the marinade). Season both sides of each pork chop with the salt and freshly ground black pepper. Working one at a time, dip each pork chop in the egg, followed by the pork rind mixture, pressing lightly to form an even coating. 4. Insert the crisper plates in each drawer, arrange the chops in a single layer in the drawers, and insert the drawers in the unit. 5. Select Zone 1 and turn the dial to select AIR FRY. Set the cooking temperature to 200°C and cook time to 12 minutes. Press the MATCH COOK button to copy Zone 1's settings to Zone 2. Press START/PAUSE to begin cooking in both zones. Air fry for 12 to 15 minutes, until crispy and a thermometer inserted into the thickest piece registers 60°C, pausing halfway through the cooking time to turn the chops. 6. Let rest for 5 minutes before serving.

Delicious Bacon Cheeseburger Meatloaf

⏰ **Prep Time: 20 minutes** 🍲 **Cook: 40-43 minutes** 🍽 **Serves: 6**

60ml beef broth
2 tablespoons heavy (whipping) cream
2½ teaspoons unflavoured gelatin
Avocado oil spray
30g chopped onion
115g keto-friendly tomato sauce
75g sugar-free mayonnaise (homemade or store-bought)
2 tablespoons keto-friendly ketchup
1 large egg, beaten
455g ground beef
Sea salt
Freshly ground black pepper
4 slices Cheddar cheese
225g sliced bacon, cooked and crumbled
1 small tomato, sliced

1. Combine the broth and heavy cream in a small bowl. Sprinkle the gelatin evenly over the top. Set aside. 2. Spray a small skillet with oil and place it over medium-high heat. Once the oil is hot, add the onion and cook for 5 minutes or until soft. 3. Reduce the heat to medium-low, then stir the gelatin mixture and add it to the skillet, along with the tomato sauce. Cook, stirring occasionally, until the mixture is reduced by half, about 10 minutes. 4. Meanwhile, stir together the mayonnaise and ketchup in a small bowl. 5. In a large bowl, combine the onion mixture with the egg and ground beef. Season with the salt and pepper. Mix well to combine. 6. Place the meatloaf mixture in a small loaf pan that fits inside your air fryer. 7. Insert a crisper plate in a drawer, place the pan in the drawer, and insert the drawer in the unit. 7. Select Zone 1 and turn the dial to select AIR FRY. Set the cooking temperature to 200°C and cook time to 20 minutes. Press the START/PAUSE button to begin cooking. 8. Top the meatloaf with the mayonnaise sauce, cheese, crumbled bacon, and tomato slices. Cook for 5 to 8 minutes more, until the cheese is melted and an instant-read thermometer reads 70°C. 9. When done, serve and enjoy.

Mustard Rosemary Pork Tenderloin with Fried Apples

⏰ **Prep Time: 10 minutes** 🍲 **Cook: 18 minutes** 🍲 **Serves: 2-3**

1 pork tenderloin (about 455g)
2 tablespoons coarse brown mustard
Salt and freshly ground black pepper
1½ teaspoons finely chopped fresh rosemary, plus sprigs for garnish
2 apples, cored and cut into 8 wedges
1 tablespoon butter, melted
1 teaspoon brown sugar

1. Cut the pork tenderloin in half so that you have two pieces that fit into the air fryer drawer. Brush the mustard onto both halves of the pork tenderloin and then season with the salt, pepper and the fresh rosemary. 2. Insert a crisper plate in a drawer, place the pork tenderloin halves in the drawer, and insert the drawer in the unit. 3. Select Zone 1 and turn the dial to select ROAST. Set the cooking temperature to 190°C and cook time to 10 minutes. Press the START/PAUSE button to begin cooking. 4. Turn the pork over and cook for another 5 to 8 minutes or until the internal temperature of the pork registers 70°C on an instant read thermometer. If your pork tenderloin is especially thick, you may need to add a minute or two, but it's better to check the pork and add time, than to overcook it. 5. Allow the pork to rest for 5 minutes. In the meantime, toss the apple wedges with the butter and brown sugar. Place the apples in the drawer and air-fry at 200°C for 8 minutes, shaking the drawer once or twice during the cooking process so the apples cook and brown evenly. 6. Slice the pork on the bias. Serve with the fried apples scattered over the top and a few sprigs of rosemary as garnish.

Steak Fajitas with Vegetables

⏰ **Prep Time: 15 minutes** 🍲 **Cook: 20-23 minutes** 🍲 **Serves: 6**

60ml avocado oil
60ml freshly squeezed lime juice
2 teaspoons minced garlic
1 tablespoon chilli powder
½ teaspoon ground cumin
Sea salt
Freshly ground black pepper
455g top sirloin steak or flank steak, thinly sliced against the grain
1 red bell pepper, cored, seeded, and cut into ½-inch slices
1 green bell pepper, cored, seeded, and cut into ½-inch slices
1 large onion, sliced

1. In a small bowl or blender, combine the avocado oil, garlic, chilli powder, lime juice, cumin, and salt and pepper to taste. 2. Place the sliced steak in a zip-top bag or shallow dish. Place the bell peppers and onion in a separate zip-top bag or dish. Pour half the marinade over the steak and the other half over the vegetables. Seal both bags and let the steak and vegetables marinate in the refrigerator for at least 1 hour or up to 4 hours. 3. Insert a crisper plate in a drawer and line the drawer with an air fryer liner or aluminium foil. Remove the vegetables from their bag or dish and shake off any excess marinade. 4. Place the vegetables in the drawer, and insert the drawer in the unit. 5. Select Zone 1 and turn the dial to select ROAST. Set the cooking temperature to 200°C and cook time to 13 minutes. Press the START/PAUSE button to begin cooking. 6. Remove the steak from its bag or dish and shake off any excess marinade. Place the steak on top of the vegetables in the drawer and cook for 7 to 10 minutes or until an instant-read thermometer reads 50°C for medium-rare (or cook to your desired doneness). 7. Serve with desired fixings, such as keto tortillas, lettuce, sour cream, avocado slices, shredded Cheddar cheese, and cilantro.

Chapter 6 Fish and Seafood

Healthy Shrimp Scampi

⏰ Prep Time: 5 minutes 🍲 Cook: 8 minutes 🥘 Serves: 4

55g unsalted butter (or butter-flavoured coconut oil for dairy-free)
2 tablespoons fish stock or chicken broth
1 tablespoon lemon juice
2 cloves garlic, minced
2 tablespoons chopped fresh basil leaves
1 tablespoon chopped fresh parsley, plus more for garnish
1 teaspoon red pepper flakes
455g large shrimp, peeled and deveined, tails removed
Fresh basil sprigs, for garnish

1. Place the butter, fish stock, garlic, basil, lemon juice, parsley, and red pepper flakes in a pan that fits your air fryer and stir to combine. 2. Insert a crisper plate in a drawer, place the pan in the drawer, and insert the drawer in the unit. 3. Select Zone 1 and turn the dial to select ROAST. Set the cooking temperature to 175°C and cook time to 3 minutes. Press the START/PAUSE button to begin cooking. Cook until fragrant and the garlic has softened. 4. Add the shrimp and stir to coat the shrimp in the sauce. Cook for 5 minutes, or until the shrimp are pink, stirring after 3 minutes. Garnish with the fresh basil sprigs and chopped parsley before serving. 5. Store leftovers in an airtight container in the refrigerator for up to 4 days. Reheat in a preheated 200°C air fryer for about 3 minutes, until heated through.

Simple Sesame-Crusted Tuna Steak

⏰ Prep Time: 5 minutes 🍲 Cook: 8 minutes 🥘 Serves: 2

2 (170g) tuna steaks
1 tablespoon coconut oil, melted
½ teaspoon garlic powder
2 teaspoons white sesame seeds
2 teaspoons black sesame seeds

1. Brush each tuna steak with the coconut oil and sprinkle with the garlic powder. 2. In a large bowl, mix sesame seeds and then press each tuna steak into them, covering the steak as completely as possible. 3. Insert a crisper plate in a drawer, place the tuna steaks in the drawer, and insert the drawer in the unit. 4. Select Zone 1 and turn the dial to select AIR FRY. Set the cooking temperature to 200°C and cook time to 8 minutes. Press the START/PAUSE button to begin cooking. Flip the steaks halfway through the cooking time. 5. Steaks will be well-done at 60°C internal temperature. Serve warm.

Crispy Crab Rangoon Patties with Sweet and Sour Sauce

⏰ **Prep Time:** 10 minutes 🍲 **Cook:** 12 minutes ▧ **Serves:** 8

Patties:
455g canned lump crabmeat, drained
1 (225g) package cream cheese, softened
1 tablespoon chopped fresh chives
1 large egg
1 teaspoon grated fresh ginger
1 clove garlic, smashed to a paste or minced
Coating:
55g pork dust
Dipping Sauce:
120ml chicken broth
80ml coconut aminos or wheat-free tamari
40g Swerve confectioners'-style sweetener or equivalent amount of liquid or powdered sweetener
60g tomato sauce
1 tablespoon coconut vinegar or apple cider vinegar
¼ teaspoon grated fresh ginger
1 clove garlic, smashed to a paste
Sliced green onions, for garnish (optional)
Fried Cauliflower Rice, for serving (optional)

1. In a medium-sized bowl, gently mix all the ingredients for the patties, without breaking up the crabmeat. 2. Form the crab mixture into eight 2½ inches in diameter and ¾ inch thick patties. 3. Place the pork dust in a shallow dish. Place each patty in the pork dust and use your hands to press the pork dust into the patties to form a crust. 4. Place bottom layer of patties in the drawer, leaving space between them. Insert the Stacked Meal Rack and place the top layer of patties on top, leaving space between them. Insert the drawer in the unit. 5. Select DOUBLE STACK PRO. Select Zone 1, select AIR FRY, and set temperature to 200°C and time to 12 minutes. Press the START/PAUSE button to begin cooking. Cook until the crust is golden and crispy. 6. While the patties cook, make the dipping sauce. In a large saucepan, whisk together all the sauce ingredients. Bring to a simmer over medium-high heat, then turn the heat down to medium until the sauce has reduced and thickened, about 5 minutes. Taste and adjust the seasonings as desired. 7. Place the patties on a serving platter, drizzle with the dipping sauce, and garnish with the sliced green onions, if desired. Serve the remaining dipping sauce on the side. Serve with the fried cauliflower rice, if desired. 8. Store leftovers in an airtight container in the refrigerator for up to 3 days. Reheat the patties in a preheated 200°C air fryer for 4 minutes, or until crispy on the outside and heated through.

Easy Pecan-Crusted Catfish

⏰ **Prep Time:** 5 minutes 🍲 **Cook:** 12 minutes ▧ **Serves:** 4

45g pecan meal
1 teaspoon fine sea salt
¼ teaspoon ground black pepper
4 (115g) catfish fillets
For Garnish (Optional):
Fresh oregano
Pecan halves

1. Insert a crisper plate in a drawer and spray the drawer with the avocado oil. 2. In a large bowl, mix the pecan meal, salt, and pepper. One at a time, dredge the catfish fillets in the mixture, coating them well. Use your hands to press the pecan meal into the fillets. Spray the fish with the avocado oil. 3. Place the coated catfish in the drawer and insert the drawer in the unit. 4. Select Zone 1 and turn the dial to select AIR FRY. Set the cooking temperature to 190°C and cook time to 12 minutes. Press the START/PAUSE button to begin cooking. Cook the coated catfish until it flakes easily and is no longer translucent in the centre, flipping halfway through. 5. Garnish with the oregano sprigs and pecan halves, if desired. 6. Store leftovers in an airtight container in the fridge for up to 3 days. Reheat in a preheated 175°C air fryer for 4 minutes, or until heated through.

Parmesan-Crusted Shrimp and Pesto Zoodles

⏱ **Prep Time:** 10 minutes   🍲 **Cook:** 7 minutes   🍃 **Serves:** 4

2 large eggs
3 cloves garlic, minced
2 teaspoons dried basil, divided
½ teaspoon fine sea salt
½ teaspoon ground black pepper
50g powdered Parmesan cheese
455g jumbo shrimp, peeled, deveined, butterflied, tails removed
Zoodles, warm, for serving
Pesto:
25g fresh basil
60ml extra-virgin olive oil or avocado oil
25g grated Parmesan cheese
30g roasted, salted walnuts (omit for nut-free)
3 cloves garlic, peeled
1 tablespoon lemon juice
½ teaspoon fine sea salt
¼ teaspoon ground black pepper

1. Insert a crisper plate in each drawer and spray the drawers with the avocado oil. 2. In a large bowl, whisk together the eggs, garlic, 1 teaspoon of the dried basil, the salt, and the pepper. In a separate small bowl, mix together the remaining teaspoon of dried basil and the Parmesan cheese. 3. Place the shrimp in the bowl with the egg mixture and use your hands to coat the shrimp. Roll one shrimp in the Parmesan mixture and press the coating onto the shrimp with your hands. Repeat with the remaining shrimp. 4. Place the shrimps in the drawers, leaving space between them, and insert the drawers in the unit. 5. Select Zone 1 and turn the dial to select AIR FRY. Set the cooking temperature to 200°C and cook time to 4 minutes. Press the MATCH COOK button to copy Zone 1's settings to Zone 2. Press START/PAUSE to begin cooking in both zones. Cook until cooked through and no longer translucent, flipping after 4 minutes. 6. While the shrimp cook, make the pesto. Place all the ingredients for the pesto in a food processor and pulse until smooth, with a few rough pieces of basil. 7. Just before serving, toss the warm zoodles with the pesto and place the shrimp on top. 8. Store leftover shrimp and pesto zoodles in separate airtight containers in the refrigerator for up to 3 days or in the freezer for up to a month. Reheat the shrimp in a preheated 200°C air fryer for 5 minutes, or until warmed through. To reheat the pesto zoodles, place them in a casserole dish that will fit your air fryer and cook at 175°C for 2 minutes, or until heated through.

Italian Baked Cod

⏱ **Prep Time:** 5 minutes   🍲 **Cook:** 12 minutes   🍃 **Serves:** 4

4 (170g) cod fillets
2 tablespoons salted butter, melted
1 teaspoon Italian seasoning
¼ teaspoon salt
125g low-carb marinara sauce

1. Place the cod into an ungreased round nonstick baking dish. Pour the butter over cod and sprinkle with the Italian seasoning and salt. Top with the marinara. 2. Insert a crisper plate in a drawer, place the dish in the drawer, and insert the drawer in the unit. 3. Select Zone 1 and turn the dial to select ROAST. Set the cooking temperature to 175°C and cook time to 12 minutes. Press the START/PAUSE button to begin cooking. 4. Fillets will be lightly browned, easily flake, and have an internal temperature of at least 60°C when done. Serve warm.

Asian Marinated Salmon

⏰ **Prep Time:** 5 minutes 🍲 **Cook:** 6 minutes 🍃 **Serves:** 2

2 (115g) salmon fillets (about 1¼ inches thick)
Sliced green onions, for garnish
Marinade:
60ml wheat-free tamari or coconut aminos
2 tablespoons lime or lemon juice
2 tablespoons sesame oil
2 tablespoons Swerve confectioners'-style sweetener, or a few drops liquid stevia
2 teaspoons grated fresh ginger
2 cloves garlic, minced
½ teaspoon ground black pepper
Sauce (Optional):
60ml beef broth
60ml wheat-free tamari
3 tablespoons Swerve confectioners'-style sweetener or equivalent amount of liquid or powdered sweetener
1 tablespoon tomato sauce
1 teaspoon stevia glycerite (optional)
⅛ teaspoon guar gum or xanthan gum (optional, for thickening)

1. In a medium-sized shallow dish, stir together all the ingredients for the marinade until well combined. Place the salmon in the marinade. Cover and refrigerate for at least 2 hours or overnight. 2. Remove the salmon fillets from the marinade. Insert a crisper plate in a drawer, place the salmon fillets in the drawer, leaving space between them, and insert the drawer in the unit. 3. Select Zone 1 and turn the dial to select AIR FRY. Set the cooking temperature to 200°C and cook time to 6 minutes. Press the START/PAUSE button to begin cooking. Cook until the salmon is cooked through and flakes easily with a fork. 4. While the salmon cooks, make the sauce, if using. Place all the sauce ingredients except the guar gum in a medium-sized bowl and stir until well combined. Taste and adjust the sweetness to your liking. While whisking slowly, add the guar gum. Let the sauce thicken for 3 to 5 minutes. (The sauce can be made up to 3 days ahead and stored in an airtight container in the fridge.) Drizzle the sauce over the salmon before serving. 5. Garnish the salmon with the sliced green onions before serving. 6. Store leftovers in an airtight container in the fridge for up to 3 days. Reheat in a preheated 175°C air fryer for 3 minutes, or until heated through.

Nutritious Fish Taco Bowl

⏰ **Prep Time:** 10 minutes 🍲 **Cook:** 12 minutes 🍃 **Serves:** 4

½ teaspoon salt
¼ teaspoon garlic powder
¼ teaspoon ground cumin
4 (115g) cod fillets
280g finely shredded green cabbage
75g mayonnaise
¼ teaspoon ground black pepper
60g chopped pickled jalapeños

1. Sprinkle the salt, garlic powder, and cumin over the cod. 2. Insert a crisper plate in a drawer, place the cod in the drawer, and insert the drawer in the unit. 3. Select Zone 1 and turn the dial to select ROAST. Set the cooking temperature to 175°C and cook time to 12 minutes. Press the START/PAUSE button to begin cooking. Turn halfway through cooking. Cod will flake easily and have an internal temperature of at least 60°C when done. 4. In a large bowl, toss the cabbage with the mayonnaise, black pepper, and jalapeños until fully coated. Serve the cod warm over the cabbage slaw on four medium plates.

Tuna Patties with Spicy Sriracha Sauce

⏱ **Prep Time:** 10 minutes 🍲 **Cook:** 10 minutes 🍴 **Serves:** 4

2 (170g) cans tuna packed in oil, drained
3 tablespoons almond flour
2 tablespoons mayonnaise
1 teaspoon dried dill
½ teaspoon onion powder
Pinch of salt and pepper
Spicy Sriracha Sauce:
55g mayonnaise
1 tablespoon sriracha sauce
1 teaspoon garlic powder

1. In a large bowl, combine the tuna, mayonnaise, dill, almond flour, and onion powder. Season to taste with the salt and freshly ground black pepper. Use a fork to stir, mashing with the back of the fork as necessary, until thoroughly combined. 2. Use an ice cream scoop to form the tuna mixture patties. 3. Insert a crisper plate in a drawer and line the drawer with parchment paper. Place the patties in a single layer in the drawer and press lightly with the bottom of the scoop to flatten into a circle about ½ inch thick. Insert the drawer in the unit. 4. Select Zone 1 and turn the dial to select AIR FRY. Set the cooking temperature to 195°C and cook time to 10 minutes. Press the START/PAUSE button to begin cooking. Cook until lightly browned, pausing halfway through the cooking time to turn the patties. 5. To make the sriracha sauce by combining the mayonnaise, sriracha, and garlic powder in a small bowl. 6. Serve the tuna patties topped with the sriracha sauce.

Crispy Fish Sticks

⏱ **Prep Time:** 15 minutes 🍲 **Cook:** 10 minutes 🍴 **Serves:** 4

30g pork rinds, finely ground
25g blanched finely ground almond flour
½ teaspoon Old Bay seasoning
1 tablespoon coconut oil
1 large egg
455g cod fillet, cut into ¾" strips

1. Place ground pork rinds, almond flour, Old Bay seasoning, and coconut oil into a large bowl and mix together. In a medium bowl, whisk egg. 2. Dip each fish stick into the egg and then gently press into the flour mixture, coating as fully and evenly as possible. 3. Insert a crisper plate in a drawer, place the fish sticks in the drawer, and insert the drawer in the unit. 4. Select Zone 1 and turn the dial to select AIR FRY. Set the cooking temperature to 200°C and cook time to 10 minutes. Press the START/PAUSE button to begin cooking. Cook until golden. 5. Serve immediately.

Authentic Green Curry Shrimp

⏰ **Prep Time:** 15 minutes 🍲 **Cook:** 5 minutes 🍽 **Serves:** 4

1 to 2 tablespoons Thai green curry paste
2 tablespoons coconut oil, melted
1 tablespoon half-and-half or coconut milk
1 teaspoon fish sauce
1 teaspoon soy sauce
1 teaspoon minced fresh ginger
1 clove garlic, minced
455g jumbo raw shrimp (21 to 25 count), peeled and deveined
5g chopped fresh Thai basil or sweet basil
5g chopped fresh cilantro

1. In a heatproof pan that fits your air fryer, combine the curry paste, coconut oil, half-and-half, fish sauce, soy sauce, ginger, and garlic. Whisk until well combined. 2. Add the shrimp and toss until well coated. Marinate at room temperature for 15 to 30 minutes. 3. Insert a crisper plate in a drawer, place the pan in the drawer, and insert the drawer in the unit. 4. Select Zone 1 and turn the dial to select AIR FRY. Set the cooking temperature to 200°C and cook time to 5 minutes. Press the START/PAUSE button to begin cooking. Stir halfway through the cooking time. 5. Transfer the shrimp to a serving bowl or platter. Garnish with the basil and cilantro. Serve and enjoy.

Tender Scallops with Lemon-Butter Sauce

⏰ **Prep Time:** 10 minutes 🍲 **Cook:** 15 minutes 🍽 **Serves:** 4

455g large sea scallops
Sea salt
Freshly ground black pepper
Avocado oil spray
55g (4 tablespoons) unsalted butter
1 tablespoon freshly squeezed lemon juice
1 teaspoon minced garlic
¼ teaspoon red pepper flakes

1. If your scallops still have the adductor muscles attached, remove them. Pat the scallops dry with a paper towel. 2. Season the scallops with the salt and pepper, then place them on a plate and refrigerate for 15 minutes. 3. Insert the crisper plates sprayed with oil in each drawer, place the scallops in a single layer in the drawers, and spray the top of the scallops with oil. Insert the drawers in the unit. 4. Select Zone 1 and turn the dial to select AIR FRY. Set the cooking temperature to 175°C and cook time to 6 minutes. Press the MATCH COOK button to copy Zone 1's settings to Zone 2. Press START/PAUSE to begin cooking in both zones. 5. Flip the scallops and cook for 6 minutes more, until an instant-read thermometer reads 60°C. 6. While the scallops cook, place the butter, garlic, lemon juice, and red pepper flakes in a small ramekin. 7. When the scallops have finished cooking, remove them from the air fryer. Place the ramekin in the air fryer and cook until the butter melts, about 3 minutes. Stir. 8. Toss the scallops with the warm butter and serve.

Cajun Salmon Burgers

⏰ **Prep Time: 40 minutes** 🍲 **Cook: 15 minutes** 🍲 **Serves: 4**

Olive oil
4 (140g) cans pink salmon in water, any skin and bones removed, drained
2 eggs, beaten
120g whole-wheat bread crumbs
4 tablespoons light mayonnaise
2 teaspoons Cajun seasoning
2 teaspoons dry mustard
4 whole-wheat buns

1. Insert a crisper plate in a drawer and spray the drawer lightly with the olive oil. 2. In a medium bowl, mix together the salmon, mayonnaise, Cajun seasoning, egg, bread crumbs, and dry mustard. Cover with plastic wrap and refrigerate for 30 minutes. 3. Shape the mixture into four ½-inch-thick patties about the same size as the buns. 4. Place the salmon patties in the drawer in a single layer and lightly spray the tops with olive oil. Insert the drawer in the unit. 5. Select Zone 1 and turn the dial to select AIR FRY. Set the cooking temperature to 180°C and cook time to 6 minutes. Press the START/PAUSE button to begin cooking. Air fry for 6 to 8 minutes. 6. Turn the patties over and lightly spray with the olive oil. Cook until crispy on the outside, 4 to 7 more minutes. 7. Serve on whole-wheat buns.

Lemon-Garlic Tilapia Fillets

⏰ **Prep Time: 10 minutes** 🍲 **Cook: 15 minutes** 🍲 **Serves: 4**

1 tablespoon lemon juice
1 tablespoon olive oil
1 teaspoon minced garlic
½ teaspoon chilli powder
4 (141g to 170g) tilapia fillets

1. Insert a crisper plate in each drawer and line the drawers with perforated air fryer liners. 2. In a large, shallow bowl, mix together the lemon juice, olive oil, garlic, and chilli powder to make a marinade. Place the tilapia fillets in the bowl and coat evenly. 3. Place the fillets in the drawer in a single layer, leaving space between each fillet. Insert the drawers in the unit. 4. Select Zone 1 and turn the dial to select AIR FRY. Set the cooking temperature to 195°C and cook time to 10 minutes. Press the MATCH COOK button to copy Zone 1's settings to Zone 2. Press START/PAUSE to begin cooking in both zones. Air fry until the fish is cooked and flakes easily with a fork, 10 to 15 minutes. 5. When done, serve and enjoy.

Chapter 7 Desserts

Keto Pecan Snowball Cookies

⏱ **Prep Time: 5 minutes** 🍴 **Cook: 24 minutes** 🎁 **Serves: 4**

120g chopped pecans
55g salted butter, melted
40g coconut flour
145g confectioners' erythritol, divided
1 teaspoon vanilla extract

1. In a food processor, blend together pecans, flour, butter, 95g erythritol, and vanilla 1 minute until a dough forms. 2. Form the dough into twelve individual cookie balls, about 1 tablespoon each. 3. Cut three pieces of parchment to fit the air fryer drawer. Place four cookies on each ungreased parchment. 4. Insert a crisper plate in the bottom of each drawer. Add one piece parchment with cookies in each drawer. Place a Stacked Meal Rack in each drawer over the cookies. Place one piece parchment with cookies on one rack and insert the drawer in Zone 1. Place one piece parchment with cookies on the other rack and insert the drawer in Zone 2. Insert the drawers in the unit. 5. Select DOUBLE STACK PRO. Select Zone 1, select BAKE, and set temperature to 160°C and time to 8 minutes. Select MATCH COOK, and then press START/PAUSE to begin cooking. 6. When the timer goes off, allow cookies to cool for 5 minutes on a large serving plate until cool enough to handle. While still warm, dust the cookies with the remaining erythritol. Allow to cool completely, about 15 minutes, before serving.

Halle Berries and Cream Cobbler

⏱ **Prep Time: 10 minutes** 🍴 **Cook: 25 minutes** 🎁 **Serves: 4**

340g cream cheese, softened
1 large egg
80g Swerve confectioners'-style sweetener or equivalent amount of powdered sweetener
½ teaspoon vanilla extract
¼ teaspoon fine sea salt
145g sliced fresh raspberries or strawberries
Biscuits:
3 large egg whites
80g blanched almond flour
1 teaspoon baking powder
2½ tablespoons very cold unsalted butter, cut into pieces
¼ teaspoon fine sea salt
Frosting:
55g cream cheese, softened
1 tablespoon Swerve confectioners'-style sweetener or equivalent amount of powdered or liquid sweetener
1 tablespoon unsweetened, unflavoured almond milk or heavy cream
Fresh raspberries or strawberries, for garnish

1. Grease a pie pan that fits your air fryer. 2. In a large mixing bowl, combine the cream cheese, egg, and sweetener with a hand mixer until smooth. Stir in the vanilla and salt. Gently add the raspberries with a rubber spatula. Pour the mixture into the prepared pan and set aside. 3. Make the biscuits. Place the egg whites in the bowl of a stand mixer or a medium-sized mixing bowl. Using a stand mixer or hand mixer, whip the egg whites until very fluffy and stiff. 4. In another medium-sized bowl, combine the almond flour and baking powder. Cut in the butter and add the salt, stirring gently to keep the butter pieces intact. 5. Gently pour the almond flour mixture into the egg whites. Scoop out the dough with a large spoon or ice cream scooper and form it into a 2-inch-wide biscuit, making sure the butter stays in separate clumps. Add the biscuit on top of the raspberry mixture in the pan. Repeat with remaining dough to make 4 biscuits. 6. Insert a crisper plate in a drawer, place the pan in the drawer, and insert the drawer in the unit. 7. Select Zone 1 and turn the dial to select BAKE. Set the cooking temperature to 200°C and cook time to 5 minutes. Press the START/PAUSE button to begin cooking. 8. Then lower the temperature to 160°C and bake for another 17 to 20 minutes, until the biscuits are golden brown. 9. While the cobbler cooks, make the frosting by placing the cream cheese in a small bowl and stirring to break it up. Stir in the sweetener. Stir in the almond milk until well combined. If you prefer a thinner frosting, add more almond milk. 10. Remove the cobbler from the air fryer and let cool slightly, then drizzle with the frosting. Garnish with the fresh raspberries. 11. Store leftovers in an airtight container in the refrigerator for up to 3 days. Reheat the cobbler in a preheated 175°C air fryer for 3 minutes, or until warmed through.

Low-Carb Chocolate Doughnut Holes

⏰ Prep Time: 10 minutes 🍲 Cook: 6 minutes 🍃 Serves: 4

110g blanched finely ground almond flour
60g low-carb vanilla protein powder
95g granular erythritol
20g unsweetened cocoa powder
½ teaspoon baking powder
2 large eggs, whisked
½ teaspoon vanilla extract

1. Mix all ingredients in a large bowl until a soft dough forms. Separate and roll dough into twenty balls, about 2 tablespoons each. 2. Cut two piece of parchment to fit your air fryer drawer. Insert the crisper plates in each drawer and line the draws with parchment paper. Place the doughnut holes in the drawers and insert the drawers in the unit. 3. Select Zone 1 and turn the dial to select BAKE. Set the cooking temperature to 195°C and cook time to 6 minutes. Press the MATCH COOK button to copy Zone 1's settings to Zone 2. Press START/PAUSE to begin cooking in both zones. Flip the doughnut holes halfway through cooking. Doughnut holes will be golden and firm when done. 4. Let cool completely before serving, about 10 minutes.

Decadent Chocolate Soufflés

⏰ Prep Time: 5 minutes 🍲 Cook: 15 minutes 🍃 Serves: 2

2 large eggs, whites and yolks separated
1 teaspoon vanilla extract
55g low-carb chocolate chips
2 teaspoons coconut oil, melted

1. In a medium bowl, beat the egg whites until stiff peaks form, about 2 minutes. Set aside. In a separate medium bowl, whisk the egg yolks and vanilla together. Set aside. 2. In a separate medium microwave-safe bowl, place the chocolate chips and drizzle with the coconut oil. Microwave on high 20 seconds, then stir and continue cooking in 10-second increments until melted, being careful not to overheat the chocolate. Let cool 1 minute. 3. Slowly pour the melted chocolate into the egg yolks and whisk until smooth. Then, slowly begin adding the egg white mixture to the chocolate mixture, about ¼ cup at a time, folding in gently. 4. Pour the mixture into two 4" ramekins greased with cooking spray. 5. Insert a crisper plate in a drawer, place the ramekins in the drawer, and insert the drawer in the unit. 6. Select Zone 1 and turn the dial to select BAKE. Set the cooking temperature to 200°C and cook time to 15 minutes. Press the START/PAUSE button to begin cooking. Soufflés will puff up while cooking and deflate a little once cooled. The centre will be set when done. 7. Let cool 10 minutes, then serve warm.

Sweet Cream Cheese Shortbread Cookies

⏰ **Prep Time:** 40 minutes 🍲 **Cook:** 20 minutes 🍮 **Serves:** 4

60ml coconut oil, melted
55g cream cheese, softened
95g granular erythritol
1 large egg, whisked
220g blanched finely ground almond flour
1 teaspoon almond extract

1. Combine all ingredients in a large bowl to form a firm ball. 2. Place the dough on a sheet of plastic wrap and roll into a 12"-long log shape. Roll the log in plastic wrap and place in a refrigerator for 30 minutes to chill. 3. Remove the log from plastic and slice into twelve equal cookies. Cut two sheets of parchment paper to fit the drawer. Place six cookies on each ungreased sheet. 4. Insert the crisper plates in each drawer, place the sheets with cookies in the drawers, and insert the drawers in the unit. 5. Select Zone 1 and turn the dial to select BAKE. Set the cooking temperature to 160°C and cook time to 10 minutes. Press the MATCH COOK button to copy Zone 1's settings to Zone 2. Press START/PAUSE to begin cooking in both zones. Turn the cookies halfway through cooking. They will be lightly golden when done. 6. Let cool 15 minutes before serving to avoid crumbling.

Tasty Olive Oil Cake

⏰ **Prep Time:** 10 minutes 🍲 **Cook:** 30 minutes 🍮 **Serves:** 8

220g blanched finely ground almond flour
5 large eggs, whisked
180ml extra-virgin olive oil
65g granular erythritol
1 teaspoon vanilla extract
1 teaspoon baking powder

1. In a large bowl, mix all ingredients. Pour the batter into an ungreased round nonstick baking dish that fits your air fryer. 2. Insert a crisper plate in a drawer, place the dish in the drawer, and insert the drawer in the unit. 3. Select Zone 1 and turn the dial to select BAKE. Set the cooking temperature to 150°C and cook time to 30 minutes. Press the START/PAUSE button to begin cooking. The cake will be golden on top and firm in the centre when done. 4. Let the cake cool in the dish for 30 minutes before slicing and serving.

Air-Fried Cinnamon Doughnut Bites

🕐 **Prep Time:** 10 minutes 🍲 **Cook:** 6 minutes 🍂 **Serves:** 4

180ml water
8 tablespoons unsalted butter, divided
4 tablespoons Swerve sugar replacement, divided
½ teaspoon salt
80g almond flour
20g coconut flour
1 teaspoon baking powder
Zest of 1 orange
2 eggs
1 teaspoon vanilla extract
2 teaspoons ground cinnamon

1. Insert a crisper plate in each drawer and line the drawers with parchment paper. Set aside. 2. In a medium pot over medium-high heat, combine the water, 2 tablespoons of the Swerve, 5 tablespoons of the butter, and the salt. Bring the mixture to boil, whisking until the butter is melted. Remove from the heat and let cool for a few minutes. 3. In a large mixing bowl, whisk together the almond flour, baking powder, coconut flour, and orange zest. Add the dry ingredients to the water mixture in the pot. Stir briskly. The mixture should be the consistency of loose mashed potatoes. 4. In a small bowl, whisk the eggs and vanilla. Add the egg mixture to the pot and whisk until smooth. Let sit for 10 to 15 minutes until the dough thickens. 5. Transfer the dough to a resealable bag. Cut a ¼-inch tip from one corner of the bag. Squeeze about 20 1½-inch mounds onto parchment paper. Freeze for 45 minutes or until hard. 6. Insert the crisper plates in each drawer, place the doughnuts in the drawers, and insert the drawers in the unit. 7. Select Zone 1 and turn the dial to select AIR FRY. Set the cooking temperature to 200°C and cook time to 6 minutes. Press the MATCH COOK button to copy Zone 1's settings to Zone 2. Press START/PAUSE to begin cooking in both zones. Air fry the doughnuts until brown and crisp. 8. In a small shallow bowl, combine the cinnamon and the remaining 2 tablespoons Swerve. In another small, shallow microwavable bowl, melt the remaining 3 tablespoons butter in the microwave on high for 30 seconds to 1 minute. 9. While the doughnuts are warm, brush with the melted butter and roll in the cinnamon-Swerve mixture. Serve warm.

Chocolate Mayo Cake

🕐 **Prep Time:** 10 minutes 🍲 **Cook:** 25 minutes 🍂 **Serves:** 6

110g blanched finely ground almond flour
55g salted butter, melted
95g plus 1 tablespoon granular erythritol
1 teaspoon vanilla extract
60g full-fat mayonnaise
20g unsweetened cocoa powder
2 large eggs

1. In a large bowl, mix all ingredients until smooth. 2. Pour the batter into a round baking pan that fits your air fryer. 3. Insert a crisper plate in a drawer, place the pan in the drawer, and insert the drawer in the unit. 4. Select Zone 1 and turn the dial to select BAKE. Set the cooking temperature to 150°C and cook time to 25 minutes. Press the START/PAUSE button to begin cooking. 5. When done, a toothpick inserted in centre will come out clean. Allow the cake to cool completely, or it will crumble when moved.

Molten Chocolate Almond Cakes

⏰ **Prep Time:** 10 minutes　🍴 **Cook:** 13 minutes　🍽 **Serves:** 3

Butter and flour for the ramekins
115g bittersweet chocolate, chopped
115g (1 stick) unsalted butter
2 eggs
2 egg yolks
50g sugar
½ teaspoon pure vanilla extract, or almond extract
1 tablespoon all-purpose flour
3 tablespoons ground almonds
8 to 12 semisweet chocolate discs (or 4 chunks of chocolate)
Cocoa powder or powdered sugar, for dusting
Toasted almonds, coarsely chopped

1. Butter and flour three (170g) ramekins. (Butter the ramekins and then coat the butter with flour by shaking it around in the ramekin and dumping out any excess.) 2. Melt the chocolate and butter together, either in the microwave or in a double boiler. In a separate bowl, beat the egg yolks, eggs, and sugar together until light and smooth. Add the vanilla extract. Whisk the chocolate mixture into the egg mixture. Stir in the flour and ground almonds. 3. Transfer the batter carefully to the buttered ramekins, filling halfway. Place two or three chocolate discs in the centre of the batter and then fill the ramekins to ½-inch below the top with the remaining batter. 4. Insert the crisper plates in each drawer, place the ramekins in the drawers, and insert the drawers in the unit. 5. Select Zone 1 and turn the dial to select BAKE. Set the cooking temperature to 165°C and cook time to 13 minutes. Press the MATCH COOK button to copy Zone 1's settings to Zone 2. Press START/PAUSE to begin cooking in both zones. The sides of the cake should be set, but the centres should be slightly soft. 6. Remove the ramekins from the air fryer and let the cakes sit for 5 minutes. 7. Run a butter knife around the edge of the ramekins and invert the cakes onto a plate. Lift the ramekin off the plate slowly and carefully so that the cake doesn't break. Dust with the cocoa powder or powdered sugar and serve with a scoop of ice cream and some coarsely chopped toasted almonds.

Mixed Berry Hand Pies

⏰ **Prep Time:** 15 minutes　🍴 **Cook:** 30 minutes　🍽 **Serves:** 4

150g sugar
½ teaspoon ground cinnamon
1 tablespoon cornstarch
150g blueberries
145g blackberries
125g raspberries, divided
1 teaspoon water
1 package refrigerated pie dough (or your own homemade pie dough)
1 egg, beaten

1. Combine the sugar, cinnamon, and cornstarch in a small saucepan. Add the blueberries, blackberries, and 60g of the raspberries. Toss the berries gently to coat them evenly. Add the teaspoon of water to the saucepan and turn the stovetop on to medium-high heat, stirring occasionally. Once the berries break down, release their juice and start to simmer (about 5 minutes), simmer for another couple of minutes and then transfer the mixture to a bowl, stir in the remaining 65g of raspberries and let it cool. 2. Cut the pie dough into four 5-inch circles and four 6-inch circles. 3. Spread the 6-inch circles on a flat surface. Divide the berry filling between all four circles. Brush the perimeter of the dough circles with a little water. Place the 5-inch circles on top of the filling and press the perimeter of the dough circles together to seal. Roll the edges of the bottom circle up over the top circle to make a crust around the filling. Press a fork around the crust to make decorative indentations and to seal the crust shut. Brush the pies with egg wash and sprinkle a little sugar on top. Poke a small hole in the centre of each pie with a paring knife to vent the dough. 4. Insert a crisper plate in each drawer and brush or spray the drawers with oil. Place two pies in each drawer and insert the drawers in the unit. 5. Select Zone 1 and turn the dial to select AIR FRY. Set the cooking temperature to 185°C and cook time to 9 minutes. Press the MATCH COOK button to copy Zone 1's settings to Zone 2. Press START/PAUSE to begin cooking in both zones. 6. Turn the pies over and air-fry for another 6 minutes. 7. Serve warm or at room temperature.

Mouthwatring S'mores Pockets

⏱ **Prep Time: 10 minutes** 🍴 **Cook: 5 minutes** 🍃 **Serves: 6**

12 sheets phyllo dough, thawed
370g butter, melted
65g graham cracker crumbs
1 (200g) Giant Hershey's milk chocolate bar
12 marshmallows, cut in half

1. Place one sheet of the phyllo on a large cutting board. Keep the rest of the phyllo sheets covered with a slightly damp, clean kitchen towel. Brush the phyllo sheet generously with some melted butter. Place a second phyllo sheet on top of the first and brush it with more butter. Repeat with one more phyllo sheet until you have a stack of 3 phyllo sheets with butter brushed between the layers. Cover the phyllo sheets with one quarter of the graham cracker crumbs leaving a 1-inch border on one of the short ends of the rectangle. Cut the phyllo sheets lengthwise into 3 strips. 2. Take 2 of the strips and crisscross them to form a cross with the empty borders at the top and to the left. Place 2 of the chocolate rectangles in the centre of the cross. Place 4 of the marshmallow halves on top of the chocolate. Now fold the pocket together by folding the bottom phyllo strip up over the chocolate and marshmallows. Then fold the right side over, then the top strip down and finally the left side over. Brush all the edges generously with melted butter to seal shut. Repeat with the next three sheets of phyllo, until all the sheets have been used. You will be able to make 2 pockets with every second batch because you will have an extra graham cracker crumb strip from the previous set of sheets. 3. Insert the crisper plates in each drawer, place the pockets in the drawers, and insert the drawers in the unit. 4. Select Zone 1 and turn the dial to select AIR FRY. Set the cooking temperature to 175°C and cook time to 4 minutes. Press the MATCH COOK button to copy Zone 1's settings to Zone 2. Press START/PAUSE to begin cooking in both zones. Air-fry for 4 to 5 minutes, until the phyllo dough is light brown in colour. Flip the pockets over halfway through the cooking process. 5. Serve warm.

Glazed Cherry Turnovers with Almonds

⏱ **Prep Time: 15 minutes** 🍴 **Cook: 14 minutes** 🍃 **Serves: 8**

2 sheets frozen puff pastry, thawed
1 (595g) can premium cherry pie filling
2 teaspoons ground cinnamon
1 egg, beaten
100g sliced almonds
120g powdered sugar
2 tablespoons milk

1. Roll a sheet of puff pastry out into a square that is approximately 10-inches by 10-inches. Cut this large square into quarters. 2. Mix the cherry pie filling and cinnamon together in a bowl. Spoon 65g of the cherry filling into the centre of each puff pastry square. Brush the perimeter of the pastry square with the egg wash. Fold one corner of the puff pastry over the cherry pie filling towards the opposite corner, forming a triangle. Seal the two edges of the pastry together with the tip of a fork, making a design with the tines. Brush the top of the turnovers with the egg wash and sprinkle sliced almonds over each one. Repeat these steps with the second sheet of puff pastry. You should have eight turnovers at the end. 3. Insert a crisper plate in the bottom of each drawer. Add two turnovers in each drawer. Place a Stacked Meal Rack in each drawer over the turnovers. Place two turnovers on one rack and insert the drawer in Zone 1. Place two turnovers on the other rack and insert the drawer in Zone 2. Insert the drawers in the unit. 4. Select DOUBLE STACK PRO. Select Zone 1, select AIR FRY, and set temperature to 185°C and time to 14 minutes. Select MATCH COOK, and then press START/ PAUSE to begin cooking. Carefully turn them over halfway through the cooking time. 5. While the turnovers are cooking, make the glaze by stirring the powdered sugar and milk together in a small bowl until smooth. Let the glaze sit for a minute so the sugar can absorb the milk. If the consistency is still too thick to drizzle, add a little more milk, a drop at a time, and stir until smooth. 6. Let the cooked cherry turnovers sit for at least 10 minutes. Then drizzle the glaze over each turnover in a zigzag motion. Serve warm or at room temperature.

Conclusion

In conclusion, the Ninja DoubleStack XL 2-Drawer Air Fryer Cookbook has been crafted to make home cooking easier, healthier, and more enjoyable. With this cookbook, you now have a vast array of recipes that cater to all tastes and occasions, helping you take full advantage of your air fryer's dual-drawer functionality. The recipes within these pages have been designed to simplify the cooking process, allowing you to prepare two dishes simultaneously without compromising on flavour, quality, or time.

Whether you're preparing a quick weekday meal, a family feast, or a treat for yourself, this cookbook's colourful, step-by-step instructions make every recipe accessible and achievable. With the Ninja DoubleStack XL 2-Drawer Air Fryer's capacity and versatility, you can experiment confidently, knowing that each dish is tailored to bring out the best in this innovative appliance. The cookbook's range of recipes covers everything from crisp snacks and nutritious mains to indulgent desserts, offering something for everyone and every dietary preference.

Beyond providing delicious recipes, this cookbook also shares practical tips on portioning, alternative ingredients, and customisation ideas, allowing you to adapt each meal to suit your family's needs and preferences. The Ninja DoubleStack XL 2-Drawer Air Fryer empowers you to create balanced, flavourful dishes with minimal effort, saving you time without compromising on taste or nutritional value.

In conclusion, the Ninja DoubleStack XL 2-Drawer Air Fryer Cookbook is a valuable tool for anyone looking to make the most of their air fryer. With its inspiring, easy-to-follow recipes and helpful insights, this cookbook will elevate your home cooking, making every meal a delightful experience. Enjoy the convenience, creativity, and joy that the Ninja DoubleStack XL 2-Drawer Air Fryer brings to your kitchen and discover just how satisfying home-cooked meals can be.

Appendix Recipes Index

Printed in Great Britain
by Amazon

54408818R00044